Sapper Dorothy

SAPPER DOROTHY LAWRENCE

Sapper Dorothy

The only English Woman Soldier
in the Royal Engineers 51st Division,
79th Tunnelling Co. during the
First World War

Dorothy Lawrence

LEONAUR

Sapper Dorothy
The only English Woman Soldier
in the Royal Engineers 51st Division,
79th Tunnelling Co. during the
First World War
by Dorothy Lawrence

First published under the titles
Sapper Dorothy Lawrence

Leonaur is an imprint
of Oakpast Ltd

Copyright in this form © 2010 Oakpast Ltd

ISBN: 978-0-85706-136-2 (hardcover)
ISBN: 978-0-85706-135-5 (softcover)

http://www.leonaur.com

Publisher's Notes

In the interests of authenticity, the spellings, grammar and place names
used have been retained from the original editions.

The opinions of the authors represent a view of events in which she
was a participant related from her own perspective,
as such the text is relevant as an historical document.

The views expressed in this book are not necessarily
those of the publisher.

Contents

A GRATEFUL TRIBUTE
TO MAN
ESPECIALLY THE BRITISH & FRENCH ALLIED
FORCES FORMERLY IN THE FIELD
AND CERTAIN INDIVIDUALS
AT HOME.

THE AUTHOR IN PRIVATE LIFE

Author's Note

I have endeavoured as far as possible in the following pages to relate the facts of my experiences as they actually occurred, but as there may be found persons who will doubt the truth of the narrative I append a letter from my chum, Sapper Dunn, whose signature has been witnessed by a Sister of the Hospital in which he was lying wounded at the time.

The original is in the hands of my publishers, as is also other evidence which I am bound in honour not to publish.

Dear Miss Lawrence,

I once more take the privilege of dropping you a few lines, hoping they find you well and hearty to receive, as it leaves me to be keeping quite well at present. Well, I have not heard anything about my operation as yet, and to tell you the truth I don't want to either, as I would like to hang on till after Christmas. Well, for the moment I did not recognize you as you came down the ward the other day. You looked so different dressed as a girl from the Royal Engineer comrade-in-arms which at Albert in September 1915 you happened to be.

When I remember you I can hardly believe, though, that three years have passed since then. It seems so short time ago since you, looking so fine as a khaki soldier, joined up in our mine-laying company, and spent ten days and nights within 400 yards from the Boche front line, under rifle fire, trench mortars and "coal boxes." Often you had to be quite alone too all through a day or a night, and we never knew what intended to fall next, did we? Sometimes all three sorts fell at once!

I think that a good many of the shells were aimed at the Albert Station; you know, the one that has been so much talked about. Anyhow, you and I used to get the benefit of them. I don't

11

believe that either you or I realized till long after quite how extraordinary it was that you never happened to get knocked out. If the sergeant had not betrayed our secret you might have seen through, as a trusted soldier, the end of the first battle of Loos as well as its early stages. I can see you now stealing along that wall by moonlight, ready to fall into line for night shift, and prepared with the Buff Regimental badge as well as R.E. equipment. Really as I think it over I cannot help laughing at what happened later on. You kept in a French convent until whatever news that you had gathered would have grown stale for use in English papers. Oh, well, you got back to Blighty in the end. Well, I think this is all that I will say at present, so I will conclude, with best wishes.

I remain, sincerely,

Sapper T. Dunn,

No. 189467, R.E.

I witness the signature of Sapper T. Dunn.

E. Warren Maunder,

Sister, Royal Berks Hospital,

Reading.

CHAPTER 1

At Creil

It was in midsummer 1915 that an English girl cycled alone into that part of the war zone situated in those days fifteen miles from the firing-line near Paris. Any girl-cyclist would have looked out of harmony with war's surroundings which marked Northern France at the time; and this particular girl-cyclist would have looked inharmonious in any possible surroundings except primæval chaos. She was a picture of unloveliness. I am that girl in question; I can make that statement!

I rode on a ramshackle cycle, priced originally "£2 a bargain" in a London shop and costing another £3 for its conveyance over the water. From that wonderful home of fashions, Paris, I rode, rigged out in an un-trimmed felt hat—though sunshine broiled the very pavements—and shabbiest of clothes, together with the largest brown-paper parcel that ever dangled behind the saddle of any lady's cycle. That overloaded cycle groaned; it joggled and rattled all along the road. At last the mudguard broke; cycle, I, and mudguard, all three groaned together. So I arrived.

The town was Creil, one of the French base camps, a centre of manufacturing industry, situated at the very foot of the war and conspicuous as one of the battlegrounds of the earliest battles. In the middle of 1915 it was sufficiently far removed from the actual fighting as to be outside the range of ordinary shells; yet across the summer air dull booms rolled both day and night. Other war notes punctuated these regular boomings; *mitrailleuse* at work and maxims that kept them company; R-ap! Ra-p! Rap! Rap R-a-rrr-p! *Mitrailleuse* crackled far away; it sounded like impatient knocks at a wooden door by human knuckles. Another sound followed. Boom! B-o-om! Heavy guns rolled their varying tones across many miles with sounds like two wooden planks colliding. Impatient rattles from startling quick-firers;

and these spasmodic noises completed the series of sound.

Through Creil the Germans had recently fought and passed out. Nothing seemed to suggest that fact. Smoke ascended from every factory chimney; few signs of mourning appeared on womenfolk to depress deeper the prevailing spirit of national sadness; young men mingled among crowds of young women in the streets; a market still filled the market-place. Everything, apparently, hummed along as usual.

I turned a corner. Jerks, not gradual phases, often mark life's progress, and one turn of a corner, here, outlined ruin from normality. Not one house appeared intact; each formed ruined walls or gaping sides; only the outside framework remained of some houses, and brick dust revealed where others had once dug deep into foundation's earth. Yet opposite in this same street unscathed houses stood; no scorch, no bullet-mark! From inquiries made, it appears that the advancing German Army, wishing only to get along rapidly, turned not aside into bystreets; they despoiled only the main line of route as they marched. Riding through these marks of European history, I looked out to find, among the medley of ruin and prosperity, some little café that would put me up. Perhaps, I thought, I can use this visit as a possible chance of penetrating nearer firing-lines than civilians ordinarily venture. I found my café. Quite a suitable *pied-à-terre* for my purpose; evidently one of those little French cafés, struggling with war, hoping to keep up its routine life of pre-war days. Instead it catered—as I saw at once— only for war's necessities. French troops swarmed around its counter and sat at its small tables; crowds came to this popular little shop.

I noticed though, as four French soldiers came in together, that not two *poilus* appeared in similar uniforms. Makeshifts they all wore, garments gathered from all quarters; strange medley of available "rigs" for Frenchmen called up so unexpectedly to the colours. One man sported such width of trousers and quaint jacket that the trousers, feeling *outre*, almost shouted their defence: "Odds! You never bought that jacket as part of the uniform to which I belong. I'm odd; or it's odd; or we're *all* odd! Anyhow I don't belong to that jacket!"

So each man's "rig-out" clashed violently in colour with himself and his marching comrade. Some *poilus* made shift with civilian articles of clothing, caps, for instance, worn at same time with uniform. In this wise France sprang to arms, ready at once in will; and ready at heart far sooner than any human power was able to complete her military equipment.

"Ah, *une petite Anglaise!*" What in the world could bring a solitary "*petite Anglaise*" to the café table of this seething French base? "*Voulez-vous une tasse de café?*" No; she politely declined "*une tasse de café.*" Strange! But would she talk as well as look on? "*Oh, avec plaisir.*" She would talk. "*C'est bien ca.*" Forthwith these dear boys and I, making a strange picture enough—an English girl with chattering crowds of French p*oilus*—talked, as hard as we could talk; discussing "*ce diable, le Boche,*" "*la guerre,*" or "*mon petit bébé chez moi et ma pauvre femme.*" ↳ German slur

A Boche undergoing in anticipation what he deserved, and the excitable *poilu* demonstrating his ultimate fate with knife and fork, over goes the "*tasse de café,*" *scalding*. And the p*oilu* instantly forgets, but only momentarily, "*la guerre,*" "*mon petit bébé,*" everything else; and the scalded knee instantly claims his excitement and voluble exclamations. Vigorously brushing his trousers, talking all the while, he mingles "*mon Dieu,*" "*café,*" "*Hélas! le sal Boche.*"

"Now, go along, you were telling me about that little *François* of yours, you know, and your home down in the South." The *poilus* here often spoke English well.

"*Oui! oui! mon petit François, il ——*"

So we regained equilibrium of mind. Vivacity of French folk! Brilliant dash of the French character! Volatile heart and volatile mind! Qualities, characteristic traits of our great Ally, that mount up in the sum-total of French character, as well as in its national achievements, far higher than human estimate truly gauges.

Eternally France "plays the foils" with any foe, be that foe Death or German brutality; when society decreed the abolition of "settling accounts" by fencing duels in the Bois de Boulogne, it left to France the spirit of fencing that belittles Germany today. In the café at Creil that spirit, demonstrating its survival, showed in trivial actions of lithe parries with forks in use as imaginary swords, and changing facial expression that skimmed momentarily over features in just such manner as the fencer changes tactics at one instant's notice Yes, the French die gracefully. English die doggedly. Americans die contentedly.

When the English girl watched these French of today, they did not happen to be dying gracefully. At that particular moment they ate—not remarkably gracefully. As already stated, Creil was a French base; there were soldiers in billets all over the town. Where I stayed these soldiers used to come, with jokes that never failed to accompany orders for drinks or hard-boiled eggs. Laughing always! And with such splendid *joie de vivre!* These men faced war as Englishmen face the

15

ring in a boxing bout. In the evening these *poilus* swarmed in, stuffed hard-boiled eggs into bulging knapsacks, sipped coffee at café tables, went out, and were next heard at daybreak, perhaps as early as four, marching on one straight road to the trenches. Occasionally familiar faces again looked in; often, far oftener they never again looked in; many found Death in those signposts that directed their steady tread, at the break of day, from smoke-swept Creil to the front-line trench fifteen miles away.

I noticed particularly that the *poilus* possessed far more pocket-money than I had expected. Despite one *sou* of pay per day, every man managed to be always spending at the base. Later I learned how wives sent regular remittances, often deducted from scanty earnings in the hayfield, ensuring comfort to the men when these husbands should leave the trenches. This sacrifice on the part of French peasantry appears usual rather than exceptional; freely it is offered as one impulse united with that embodied spirit of France in which Frenchwomen offer their sons to reinforce the battlefield of beautiful France. Frenchwomen do it as a matter of course. Frenchwomen at Creil were typical of French womanhood as a whole. They worked incessantly. But in all the heat of industry they kept going all their domestic duties. Peasants at Creil calmly continued preparing *dejeuner* in kitchens where the walls were only kept up by wooden planks thrust against the sides.

Suddenly some newsboy would come past the door with his cries of the latest war-news. Soldiers flocked out towards this lad. He turned out to be a *coster*, displaying glaring maps on the backs of which appeared all the comic songs in vogue among the troops. He earned his *centimes*, passed on his way and hallooed farther up the street. Excitement evaporated. Once more "*la petite Anglaise*" attracted attention. How did she come in this unusual manner? Not a nurse! Not a uniformed worker, then why here? I explained I wanted to look around; and just a few won my confidence enough for me to say, "I want to go right into the firing-line." At least one man suggested that I should go there as a French *poilu*. Unhappily my English accent might perhaps betray identity; acquaintances and I abandoned that idea.

Owing to the fact that often there came to the café men who could speak English fluently, through their kindness I was enabled to see far more of Creil than otherwise would have proved to be possible. At first it was necessary for me to make one point quite clear. My *poilu* friends really must not make love! "*La petite Anglaise*" preferred that they should refrain from these little temptations. After that, black-bearded Southerners, blue-eyed French boys, and the little English girl got on famously together.

We all sat (fishing), for instance, on the same bank. I usually caught nothing, despite worms put on for me, time after time, except a cold in my inside!

The shop windows at Creil varied between displays of prosperous trade and straw-strewn floors. Shops had been commandeered; French soldiers lay billeted on their floors. Goods sold rapidly from other shops that managed to cater in any way for the war. Sentinels guarded bridges that spanned the narrow river; and sentinels barred the high-way at every turn of the road. But in the market-place life went on as usual. Venders said, however, how living expenses for a peasant exceeded by £1 a month their cost price at the outbreak of hostilities; and it was only at that time midsummer of 1915. Undersized cabbages cost 2d. each. None of the indispensable commodities seemed out of stock; I felt unprepared for that fact when I visited the marketplace.

Exorbitant prices were the general rule. Meat had gone up 5d. a lb. since the war; butter sold at 1s 11d. per lb.; and even Camembert cheeses cost 10d., and not 7d. each. Oddly enough, homegrown pears cost double pre-war prices, dearer than certain imported food. Carrots sold no longer in bunches, but fetched 1d each; and haricot beans cost double the usual price in 1915, though they form one of the staple French foods. Fish was particularly expenive.

In spite of every difficulty, Creil market kept cheerful. Venders stoically resigned themselves to customers who had grown fussier than ever with money that must do double its usual duty. Somehow barrows kept full with supplies; and people lived tolerably on well-prepared soups; less meat; vegetable concoctions; fruit both stewed and raw; home-made jams; *café au lait;* cream cheeses light wines; artichokes and cream. Every one appeared healthy, except for his bad teeth. Hardly anyone possessed a complete set of natural dentals! And drinking water must be held responsible, I was told, for the decay that set in unusually early despite the naturally good teeth.

Land was kept under good cultivation. Any hour of the day showed entire families working in the fields; invalided soldiers tilled the soil and middle-aged women, together with old men, bent double with age, shared alike the toil of the fields. Babies sprawled amongst these people—cooing, seated there in fields where parents threw shawls for their use on the ground. Public gardens seemed in good order, with lawns trimmed and bright flowers outlining every border. Six months

[margin note: town images? juxta-positioning]

17

earlier the Boches fought fiercely by the very houses of this prospering town. Humble cottagers had not slipped into war-panic; their little homes looked much as usual; baskets, brilliant with geraniums, swung in the wind outside each homestead. Shops kept open. Hosiery, however, had gone up terribly; cotton scarcity caused skirts and velvet materials to be extremely expensive. No firm had shut down on account of bankruptcy; despite all its trials the little place kept its flag flying. Men occupied their leisure in fishing; hardly ever did I see anyone drunk.

In the midst of this quiet life, war opened fire. With the screech of a motor siren, red-tabbed English officers flashed past and into the open country *en route* for the front. They hardly missed, in that rapid progress, an endless line of heavy lorries, stacked with munitions, *en route* for the same destination. Again another noise, heavy crashing vibrated across the dull summer air. "*Hélas! Hélas!*" cried the little Frenchwoman. Fritz bombards ——, a town five miles distant. She never stopped, however, handing stoically across the counter relay after relay of hard-boiled eggs!

Six o'clock each evening marked another war sensation; at that hour the little railway station, bristling with agitation, witnessed ambulances that crowded along the kerb to take heavy cases as far as Royaumont Hospital; and slight cases, refreshed by hot drinks, handed out by English ladies, benefited through the movable canteen established for their use. So often Sisters of Mercy passed in rough wagons on their way to succour dying soldiers at distant hospitals, while, near these solitary forms of gentle nurses, there marched at times the contrasting sight of begrimed soldiers, laughing, and on the march in brightly-hued uniforms splashed with war-horror! Going through Creil, these men passed officers, seated at café tables, playing dominoes as recreation on "rest" days. Officers appeared as "paying guests" at one *franc* daily; soldiers were billeted at State charges.

Excellent feeling existed between the civilians and the military under the unusual experience of a manufacturing town flooded with *pioupious*. Ranks appeared amenable to authority; there was, apparently, no sign of drunkenness or disorder. *Patronnes* at cafés sought to "mother" these French soldiers, and, temporarily at least, these *patronnes* in their turn received regard as little mothers. Every type of man, as applying to appearance, dropped in sooner or later at one café or another; youthful, fair-haired *pioupious* marched side by side with black-bearded Southerners, veterans of service in '70, and occasionally

18

full-breeched and befezzed Turcos joined the throng.

These men talked in those days often about their absent families, unexpected separation often divided children from mothers, also sisters from their little brothers. One of the railway *employés* said that the Germans, having invaded the *département* where he had lived, left him with *no* idea where his wife and children found refuge!

Everyday-life at Creil outlined that distinction between Frenchmen and French womenfolk which has gone far to carry France through every time of national peril. Frenchwomen are not by any means emotional; at least this is true in time of war. All misfortunes they accept with calm stoicism, not unmixed with sheer indifference. "*C'est la guerre*"; and that explains everything. Oftener than not Frenchwomen do not leave off "making their kitchens" long enough to offer brief explanation. Frenchmen become far more emotional under stress of excitement; happily their excitement takes form as laughter, song, *les blagues,* and throughout peals of the "*Marseillaise*" ring from voices that echo to the world from the united soul of a great people. National characteristics became very clear in the busy manufacturing centre, where troops raised clouds of dust in marching to the front, factory chimneys sent up dark wreaths of smoke where factories filed heavy war-munitions, and trade went on, though Germany thunder at the gate. Germany had already made deep havoc.

Three times weekly that splendid hospital at Royaumont sent in to Creil for cartloads of provisions. A khaki-clad Englishwoman always drove to market, taking with her a male khaki-clad assistant; the lady alone made selections for all necessary purchases. How splendid she looked, this jolly Englishwoman, hoisted on sacks of potatoes on which she sat to shout orders! She helped to haul under cover heavy sacks of potatoes and carrots and meat, driving away from the market as soon as she had got from it all that was best there! Everyone knew this khaki lady, not excepting venders of cheap war-souvenirs; and occasionally her assistant bought her a toy *képi* or golliwog and laughingly handed up these trophies over that exalted seat of potatoes! Sellers plied ready trade in model toy "military water-bottles" and model *képis.*

Conducted one day over one of the munition factories, I saw the latest French war inventions under experiment. Machinery turned out steel bars, varying between massive rods, thicker than a man's arm, and slender rams appearing frailer than ordinary lead pencils. In large rooms sounded throbs from revolving cylinders; apparatus perpetually revolved molten metal; and other machinery noisily bored, clipped, chopped, and sectioned. This sort of work represented the occupation of nearly every male worker at Creil in these days; indeed, Creil ranks as one of the chief manufacturing centres in Northern France. Life in it typifies life in all surrounding districts.

For this reason I wished for other experiences at Senlis; there Germans had not long ago fought and pillaged. I applied for *sauf-conduit*, permitting brief visits to Senlis. Readily this was granted. So, jumping on my cycle one lovely afternoon, I made off towards Senlis. Soldiers waved *au revoir* from the café where I had stayed; my old parcel joggled along behind the saddle; and a long fishing-rod extended itself full-length down my back! This rod stretched out beyond my head and only managed to skirt the back wheel of my cycle! Thus I departed.

CHAPTER 2

Sleeping in Senlis Forests

I rode several miles before I reached my destination. Along smooth avenues in white and dusty breadth, one goes ahead for miles on the roads of this district without curving and on ground of stoneless regularity. One winter of war, however, sufficed to stamp occasional deep furrows, interrupting that usual evenness with narrow channels of dip-down that indicated where wagon-trails travelled over slushy soil. So munition wagons left their mark.

As I passed, one long trail of these wagons grunted their way towards the fighting zone; and children lined up one side to throw delicate harebells, which clung wistfully on open iron-jaws of some projecting munition; and dying anemones, falling from childish hands, oozed slowly their last drops, as heavy wheels passed over the delicate petals of these wild flowers. And then the wagons rolled on. *Poilus* poked out their heads as their wagons went by, flinging out some ready jest. One side of war this is; yes, and *one* side only.

Nothing very eventful happened on my Senlis journey[on previous rides I had found diversion by brief lessons in musketry, gladly given by French soldiers while they mended old rifles at the wayside.]There is quite a perceptible difference in touch between English-made rifles and rifles in use by our French comrades; the French weapon weighs heavier, appears less modern, and feels clumsier to handle.

Frequently my cumbersome parcel became lop-sided; its weight overbalanced itself and me! Eventually we both came off unceremoniously in the middle of the road. Just a bit of a dust! Nothing more. And I picked myself up, together with cycle and bundle, and started on again. Maybe this little exercise occurred five times on the road to Senlis! Perhaps spectators mistook me for a cyclist acrobat intent on practising his tricks. On my arrival at Senlis, I saw how terribly it revealed the shattering achieved by recent German invasion. Entire streets lay in heaps of bricks and mortar; yet, again, as in Creil, opposite, houses intact faced these signs of ruin. Ridiculous little evidences of war, not without their mute, pathetic appeal, crossed one's path at every turn. Here, a signboard, stating that haircutting could be done at this shop, jutted outwards to the road from a mere mound of bricks. These bricks were all that remained of the shop that the signboard once faithfully described.

Elsewhere sat such articles as berusted tin kettles with spouts bespattered with brick-dust. Senlis railway station looked, perhaps, most remarkable of all this ruin; portions of its woodwork appeared scarcely touched, while treble rows of window frames gaped with empty edges on which not one pane of glass remained.

Occasionally war refrains from ravaging; it makes ruin with a precision of detail worthy, through its neatness of workmanship, to vie with any fine needlework done by aged spinsters' hands! Spectators of that Senlis station might easily believe that only glaziers' skill had removed all the windows from the station; really a shell formed the chisel that cut out, with nicety of touch, each pane of window glass.

Trains ran as usual from the station; and, indeed, life as usual prevailed in this neighbourhood. It seemed strangely quiet here, in this agricultural district, as compared with the bustle of life, significant of the neighbouring factory town. Yet—row upon row stood those plain wooden crosses. Among them "To an unknown Soldier"; here and there stood crosses that lacked any record of name or regiment. Mighty little row of "contemptibles," standing stiffly to attention, as sunshine or rain touched each with Nature's varying glory in perpetual benediction.

"Over there, in that corner, lies our *maire*," said one of the townsfolk. So quietly at rest lay that brave mayor; shot ruthlessly, as all the world knows—the victim of German savagery. "They took him out and just shot him." That was all. Not far off spread one of the earlier battlefields, situated hardly outside the town. Nothing gory marked its area. Mercifully, Nature heals her wounds quickly. Grass already covered the shell-holes, green leaves sheltered the places only lately laid open. One revolting scene of butchery occurred at this place, holding yet its mementoes of crime, in a cottage on a road that led from Senlis to the country. Sticking out, among a heap of ruins, an iron leg of a bedstead rusted in all weather. This was pointed out to me.

"You see that bed?" said a villager.

I nodded.

"On that bed they roasted alive a bedridden old woman, after pouring kerosene oil upon her and the cottage."

He knew full details, this man. It happened that the victim had been his mother-in-law. He had fled from the invasion, taking with him both wife and child. On his return eyewitnesses related what had happened. In justice let it be said, however, that the general confusion attendant on bombardment tends to minimize the powers of observation of villagers who stand in danger of instant death.

Apparently German behaviour varied between treatment of their civilian foes that would make Nero blush and the cold indifference of conquering hosts.

"They merely marched in here," said some townspeople,—though not at Senlis,— "ordered food, ate it, and marched out again."

Other people said:

"Oh, they just made themselves quite at home. They took what they wanted."

Elsewhere, wholesale murder formed the order of the day.

The recuperative energy possessed by French people in a singularly strong degree makes it possible for France to recover speedily from her worst blows. And their calm stoicism, so peculiarly French, makes Frenchwomen heroines in time of war. Mark that leave-taking of the *poilu*. Here let me briefly describe it. I happened to be in a French home when its master returned to the trenches. There was celebrated a family feast before the *soldat* started off, to which his brothers-in-law with their families came, as well as his own people. Conversation grew rather significant.

"I hope I shan't be maimed," said the young husband, glowing at that time with health and youth. "Die, far rather." Adding, "*Oui! ma petite,*" as the wife protested. "You think now that you'd love me just the same if I came home legless or armless. But think of it! Maimed! No! As years passed you'd grow to feel I was a burden."

In those words this man voiced what thousands feel, both English and French, on both sides of the Channel. Happily, men never understand women; they do not realize that maimed men win deepened love, with its maternal instinct, from their womenfolk. He got up from the table, disappeared into the other room, leaving the door half-open. There he took his wife in his arms; then walked out of the flat. At his wish, his wife did not even go to the window as he walked up the street; instead, she passed into the little kitchen and started washing up the tea-things! Typical picture, this; it stands for French homes to-ay.

Only two nights elapsed before I was told that I must leave Senlis, my *sauf-conduit* expiring after forty-eight hours' stay there.

During my brief visit, *gendarmes* grew very active on my behalf. I passed about half my time under arrest or regaining freedom! If I cycled two miles out, I was promptly arrested and brought back again! If I talked with villagers at their doorsteps, I found that a *gendarme* kept his eye on me all the time! In the whole list of French officials no one renders truer service than the *gendarme*. Spies! Why, he seems to sleep with that word written on his brain!

On being told that I must quit, I had not the slightest intention of obeying! I became, instead, a gipsy. When leaving England, I had brought with me a big white linen bag, marked "Linen" in green silk letters; into this bag I stuffed provisions as soon as I knew I must make myself scarce from Senlis. Higgledy-piggledy I put into that bag spirit-lamp, bread, candle, butter, matches, eggs, saucepan, and a bottle of water. And they jangled all together. I then tramped away, leaving my cycle hidden under a shed. For several miles I walked. I left Senlis on one of those nights when moonlight dodges darkness, shifting magic pictures across every vale and cranny. I passed along a road with ruined houses on one side, unharmed buildings on the other; it was a long road, gradually trailing off into the open country. How silent it was that night!

My footsteps made a ghostly echo through the ruins of these recent horrors. And that bed-leg stood up eerily in the moonlight as I passed by the ruined place; flitting shadows dodged first on one bit of ruin then on another, and crumbling walls stood stark against the sky-line. No dog barked. No human voice sounded. There abode the horror of a great silence; and what in life further intensifies ruin than silence brooding over it? Gradually, as I walked, houses grew scarcer; after two hours I got to open fields. It grew steadily darker. It was difficult to make out my bearings. Towards midnight I arrived at the forests that border Senlis. Tall pines darted skywards, so close together that, had it been daylight, one could not have seen the sky; under my feet, as I walked, dead leaves crackled fearsomely through this wonderful silence. I sat down.

Overhead the dense pines appeared to dwarf any living human figure. Suddenly heavy booms rent the air; and guns bellowed—evidently very near at hand. So here I was! Here, under gunfire, alone at midnight, in this weird forest! Plunging my hand into my bag I felt

THE AUTHOR IN SENLIS FORESTS

among stove and bread till I caught hold of a candle. This I pulled out.
I then set it up among the leaves on the ground. Lighting the spirit-
stove that I pulled out next, I proceeded to prepare supper by boiling
an egg in water; and this water I intended to use later for cocoa. But
the candle would persist in wobbling over!

And I heard sounds; yes, unmistakable sounds, though no creature
came through this pitch darkness. These sounds continued; but I could
only see those straight old trees as they shot skywards. Later I realized
that forests never sleep; teeming life keeps them ever wakeful. Here,
invisible beasts made pleasant chorus in their myriads; a steady purring
and whirring sound they made, while, belching only ten miles away,
cannons occasionally killed this chorus by boom! boom! boom! As
though to punctuate, there set in a quick tap! tap! tap! *Mitrailleuse!* I
could not sleep. Rats came to investigate me. Squirrels scuttled up for
a look. Invisible little beasties heaved up my leafy bed with an accompaniment of purrings, cracklings, and creakings. All those countless
sounds made chorus within the world of animal life that composes a
forest's population of animals, beasts, and insects.

And the cold! Oh, never, never shall I forget how intensely cold
those nights can be, those nights that follow hot summer days. By 3
a.m. cold penetrated my very bones. Despite my covering of blanket
coat, cold seemed to freeze my blood. No one could have persuaded
me that midsummer nights in forests could be so utterly cold. It was
incredible! How thankful I felt, as I walked about in the gloom, when
shafts of moonlight pierced those massed trees, and one little robin
perched in the grey dawn of early morning to sing his breakfast carol
on the borders of the forest.

In ever such a hurry I picked up my linen bag and away I went. I
made towards the river, far from forests, hoping to bathe before any
agricultural workers started their labours in the fields. Disappointment
met me. Already men were guiding machines over the rich fields. And
I ran the risk of being caught by these men as I bathed—they might
turn towards the river at any minute. I postponed my dip. Instead of
it I took a picnic breakfast, followed by a journey to the river, with
my fishing-rod. Somehow I hoped I might catch my dinner from that
river; it happened to be noted for its fine fish. By this time I found
myself practically without money.

Soon I was joined by a French officer. He fished. And he gave me
experienced aid. Together we managed to catch half a dozen poor
gasping creatures, each about the size of swollen minnows! I became

27

possessed of the joint catch; and later it made my dinner. Farther down the river I dared not venture; that vigilant *gendarme* certainly intended to catch sight of me. So I walked about for some hours, and fished again. Thus passed another day. Night drew on; with it I must make new plans. No more forest beds; they were too cold! I decided on cornfields in place of forests. Cornstacks dotted every field; about five bundles formed one stack. Under one stack I could surely manage to conceal myself. Anyhow I resolved to try. I proceeded to a selected stack; and arrived at it when the shadows began to fall. Thrusting aside sheaves of barley I managed to crawl into the middle; here, barricaded by corn, I started preparation for the evening meal. Lighting up the spirit-lamp, I managed to get some heat into cocoa and water. I drank this mixture.

I pushed myself farther into the stack, gathered up my knees under my chin, pulled one sheaf over the aperture I had made and then I tried for sleep. Oh, the buzzing that went on within the cornstack! It was fifty times worse than the noises in that forest! Myriads of tiny, invisible insects sat congregationally over their evening prayers. Or was it quarrelling? None told which it was! Anyhow they talked. Meanwhile I became one living mass of swollen bites. Harvest bugs, I suppose. Stifling heat set up in this compressed space; and I could not rest five minutes. I stayed there, though; I dared not go into the town, unless as a passing traveller *en route* for some given place. I had to remain among these fields or be vanquished in my exploit of getting to the front. Of fields or failure, I preferred fields, so I stayed where I lay. Up till now I had obtained no means of getting nearer the fighting line.

And it was in order that I should get to the front that I endured insects, heat, delayed baths, and vigilant gendarmes. No information likely to help my project had come so far. In view of this fact I resolved, therefore, on returning to Paris. There I hoped, perhaps, that further opportunities might arise for getting "out there"; on this mission I intended to take risks in order to test very many of Life's applied principles; hence, after a second night in those cornfields, I set forth for Paris once more.

CHAPTER 3

In Soldier's Clothes

In August 1915 the city of Paris was no longer in a state of paralysis. The sudden cessation of normal life at the outbreak of war had given place to intense activity, with war-work as its pivot; every Parisian was busy, and idle visitors either became rapidly absorbed into that great working machine or fled from Paris, inspired to flight by sheer loneliness amid this scene of life. Never had those wonderful boulevards appeared fuller with martial splendour than when, in the scorching sun of this hot summer, khaki lads, side by side with blue-uniformed French troops—all spending their brief leaves in Paris—sat together outside cafés.

Along the main thoroughfares one passed shuttered shops with "*Mobilisé*" written outside, occasionally interrupting the continuous line of business houses. Swiftly travelling along these broad roads, Red Cross cars skirted other traffic, pavements swarmed blue with the weather-soiled uniforms of French soldiers. Each evening the main Parisian stations let down their gangways for long lines of troops, men come home for short leave; and mothers and sisters passed along the kerb to greet their loved ones. Throughout six weeks I had watched these scenes daily; and my resolve grew with the weeks in determination to get "out there."

On that June afternoon when the English Channel boat glided gently out from harbour, accompanied by the usual rope-creaking and first lift of the great anchor, I felt, as the stretches of grey-blue water widened between England's mainland and our boat, a queer presentiment that adventures lay in store for me; I wondered whether I should set foot again in this country. "Perhaps I shall never come back. Anyhow I mean to get into the very thick of it. And if I die or if I am killed, well, I die, that's all; I live; and my corruptible hide simply

29

mindset / quote

parts company with me."

Thus I spoke to myself, adding: "I'll see what an ordinary English girl, without credentials or money, can accomplish. If war-correspondents cannot get out there, I'll see whether I cannot go one better than these big men with their cars, credentials, and money. I'll see what I can manage as a war-correspondent!" In those words lay the drift of my thoughts.

"Please just give me the barest means of getting out there; that is, permission to use the name of the paper. I don't want a big salary! Just give me enough to *get* there, leave the rest to me." So I pleaded with each big London paper, unavailingly.

"Nonsense, *of course* not. Do you suppose we're going to send a woman out there when even our own war-correspondents can't get out for love or money?"

It happened that a very fine paper passed that remark. Yes, it seemed reasonable enough! Some of the most renowned war-correspondents in the world, worthy of respect, as honourable individuals, whom it was hoped that the War Office might trust enough to allow *reasonable* facilities, subject rightly to military veto—these men kicked their heels while railing at senseless Fate; and Rolls-Royce cars puffed outside, unable to run their owners to Victoria Station *en route* for the front.

"Of course if you could get to the *front,* well, then it *would* ——" incomplete sentence never finished—said a certain news editor, speaking heedlessly without the slightest notion of conveying definite orders.

"I'm hanged if I won't try," thought I. To my lasting regret I failed as a war-correspondent, promises made subsequently to the War Office cut out any usefulness in that direction.

Under certain conditions newspapers rule the fate of nations; events in this war reveal this as an incontrovertible fact. One newspaper in England practically turned the tide, in the years 1914-18, that swept into obloquy the fate of the proud Hohenzollern race and freed the life of the Allied nations. In that perpetually moving invisible machinery of the World's mind, newspapers, recluses emerging day or night from dark revolving cylinders in rooms buried far back in narrow little Fleet Street, silently tilted crowns from sovereign heads and recast *personæ* in the world's ceaseless drama. Pulse of the world recording the whole life of that great body in one concentrated beat! So to the mind of the writer appears any dominating newspaper; by day and night gathering its news, like life-blood in perpetual flux, and varying with

30

the World's day; it then concentrates the whole by morning edition or evening edition, representing, as it were, within that fold of printed matter called "newspaper" the beat of the great World's pulse.

Arrived again in Paris, I renewed my efforts to find likely opportunities of help for getting away. Two assets came in usefully. By instinct I know whether a man is trustworthy from a woman's point of view, whether he is likely to take any advantage of her. I can rely equally well on the instinctive power that tells me for what work individual men happen naturally to be suited. Those two assets have been useful to me throughout life; and never more useful than on the occasion of this great adventure.

From Paris cafés I chose my first two male assistants. Two khaki soldiers, two amongst thousands with which Paris appeared flooded, soldiers with faces of clean-minded boys; they sat with rather lonesome expressions opposite one of the Paris railway stations. "They'll do," I said. By flashes I pick units for any organization which I undertake, success depends wholly on types and the personalities in each type. In absolute frankness I spoke to each man in the tone of an Englishwoman who salutes a fellow-countryman. No one here in England can imagine with what wistful longing those khaki men out there wish for even the tiniest bit of home. Just to speak with an English girl means home grown nearer. I knew their feelings. And I knew those two seated in the café" represented men who happened to be the sort who badly wanted any bit of home.

"Hullo! boys," I said.

They looked up in surprise; but very soon we three were talking and laughing together at the table. How wholesomely glad these men felt to see "one of us"! We talked about home. Soon I learnt exactly how many children one man possessed—nine, as it happened—and that his bachelor mate had come home recently from India. For five minutes, these khaki boys wondered, I admit, whether I was "out for love"! Of their own accord they soon put that idea out of their heads. Before we had talked for a quarter of an hour I said bluntly:

"I want to get out to the front as a soldier. Will you help me?" They looked at me.

"But what do you want us to do?"

"Well, the first essential means uniform, doesn't it?" I replied.

About this time there appeared no scarcity of spare uniforms, and several fairly good specimens happened to be about the place where these lads were billeted. My two new acquaintances, struck with the spirit of sport afforded by this adventure, agreed straight away to help. They undertook to find my outfit; it must consist of jacket, badge, cap, puttees, shirt, and boots. No light matter for two privates to supply. In subsequent meetings I tried in return to offer them some slight token of my gratitude, showing my companions round Paris and giving whatever scant hospitality lay within my quickly emptying purse.

"How is this outfit to change hands without arousing suspicion?" I asked.

"Let them think it is our washing."

I might say that Frenchwomen usually did Tommy's washing, and he used to bring it out, wrapped in paper. My new friends said:

"Every night we'll come out with our washing, wrapped in newspaper, and you must take it from us. By degrees we'll get you everything."

Regularly after that I used to meet the men under the trees of a famous boulevard, and the "washing" changed hands there.

"Hullo, Bill, what yer got there?" asked a comrade.

"Only the washing."

Surprising how much "linen" can leave one billet from two men in a week! The great wash happened to be a pair of military boots; the second wash consisted of khaki trousers; whilst the third newspaper parcel to change hands under those trees turned out braces, jacket, cap, shirt, and *puttees* So much for that week's wash! What a lark! How a dear old C.O. would have sworn or laughed! This outfit came into my possession without more ado than "Goodnight from passing soldiers. I would approach, be saluted; walk a little way; and then hoist under my arm a parcel, as I lumped on my cycle, riding away through the growing dusk I rode straight to my hotel, situated on the outskirts of Paris. On arrival I tried on these clothes in my room.

Reader, have you ever attempted to incline trousers in the way that they should go on a female figure? They do not know the way, and suddenly you realize that neither do you! Unfortunately I could not decently call in masculine assistance; whereas I suffered the usual ignorance of "only child and orphan" who never sees brothers' discarded "brigs." I was left alone to struggle with unknown buttons, braces, and the division sum of how to make a big body go into a small size of trousers! Eventually I got in by a series of jumps, jerks, and general tightening up! *Puttees* proved equally refractory; and I had to postpone putting them on until I could be taught what to do.

My third difficulty was how to discover some means of reducing my robust figure to masculine slimness. I managed it this way. Enveloping myself in swathes of bandages, like a mummy, I pulled these swathes taut around my body, after the removal of all ordinary attire. Even then the waistline showed above the dip of my back. So I padded my back with layers of cotton wool. Then my shoulders outlined the division between my back and the padding! I finished by making, out of sacking, a big apron, which, suspended by strings, I slung down my back, fixing it over layers of wool, thus making of my back one flat surface. In final effect my outfit might deceive any eye; it revealed a thick-set and plump figure, finished by a somewhat small head and a boyish face. Here stood some English boy, hardly more than eighteen years of age. *(disguising female figure)*

"We don't mind helping you, kiddy," said the khaki men. "You'll never get near enough to be in danger." *Sport? entertainment?*

Later, I paraded under the trees in the boulevards, actually in uniform, if I remember rightly, accompanied by the two real soldiers who met me at the gates of Paris; they walked beside me, marshalling me along the boulevards while instruction took place in military drill and correct step. *(military lessons)*

Not many days subsequent to these performances there occurred what I felt might mean doom to all my hopes. The *patron* of the hotel where I stayed discovered my uniform! Carelessly going out, without locking my bedroom door, I left my precious uniform in the cupboard. On my return, later in the day, I discovered in a wineglass, placed on my table, just one scrap of brown paper, bearing an address, that had been torn off my paper parcel. Horrors! Someone had opened that cupboard door. All my little plans seemed to collapse as I picked up that bit of paper with its address. What an awful moment I endured! Then I recovered; I went straight with it to the *patron*!

"Someone has been in my room. This is what I have found," I exclaimed.

But his face looked quite blank.

"I can't read that address," he replied. We looked at each other squarely; a smile crept over his face, and he added, "That's a lesson for you never to leave your door unlocked when you stay in an hotel. I am the culprit. And I just did that to give you a lesson."

Later I found what true "sporty "friends I had in the *patron* and his wife; neither gave away my secret; and when I did cycle off for the front I chose as one of my "accomplices" our *patron*, who fastened on with his own hands the incriminating uniform behind my cycle.

(hotel owner as central ally)

Quite frankly I confided to the *patron* my intentions; and he helped them along in every innocent way.

Though I had my uniform I appeared as far as ever from the fulfilment of my dreams. I had no passport. I saw no means of getting one. My khaki friends, two of the Leicester Regiment, said:

"If you can get to Béthune you will be all right. From there you can easily get on to the trenches."

"Yes, but I cannot get there. Béthune is the front of the front; no civilian may go there. Even in soldier's uniform I could not go without a pass from headquarters."

Hours of cogitation followed this announcement; it faced the latest dilemma. At last solutions seemed to be coming through.

"You can make out that for yourself," said my two comrades. "Write," they directed. And I wrote:

PASS

forging documents + knowledge

Private Denis Smith has leave to be absent from his quarters from August 16th till August 23rd on special business.

Signed———, Commanding Officer,

1st Leicestershire Regiment.

It had become customary for private soldiers to make out their own passes, leaving only space for the signature of the C.O. My handwriting easily adjusts itself to suit any hand; and I wrote out the pass and the blank without difficulty. In selecting a name for the signature, I chose what happened to be fictitious, thus avoiding all semblance of forgery. To get the stamped impress of headquarters' stamp, I purchased a disc from a cycle shop which, tempered with marking ink, might give the desired effect. This done I was rehearsed by my friends—who knew Béthune—in the names of the officers belonging to "my" regiment; where I must say I had come from, if questioned; which troops would share my billet; and how and where to join my regiment. I tried to get a pay-book, also identification disc, in case of death. Though I got my disc, I had to manage without any pay-book. My disc, reading as follows: "D. Smith No. 175331, 1st Leicester Regt. R.C." (meaning Roman Catholic, though I am not a Roman Catholic in civilian life), was formed of brown leather. I hung it round my neck, as was customary.

Suddenly it occurred to me that I would make a very bold venture. As a civilian, I would apply, after the usual manner, for a passport to

(not disguised)

Calais via the town at the front to which I wished to go. My hair had not yet been cropped; and I looked, when out of uniform, like a rather poor English girl. I called on the local French *maire;* part of his work in wartime involved the signing of passports, or rather *sauf-conduits.* The dear old Frenchman greeted me with a gracious smile and a bow; I had spent a little time in his town.

"I'm leaving here in a few days," I said. "And as I have a bicycle I want to cycle as far as Calais, rather than train there."

He listened attentively.

"You are leaving our beautiful France so soon? Can't you stay longer?" He smiled kindly.

"Unfortunately I must be off, I fear," I replied. "But I have enjoyed my visit immensely. Perhaps you will give me a pass to train as far as Amiens; then I can cycle on to Calais. It is rather a long cycle-ride from here to Calais."

The old Frenchman sat down at his desk, took up a pen, and began to write. He wrote my name. "*Cheveux?* Blonds," he wrote.

"Travelling where?"

"Calais." Taking my courage in both hands I added, though in an off-hand manner, as I looked over his shoulder, "*via* Béthune. I think I'll go that way as I have friends there."

He paused with his pen in mid-air, then he said:

"Ah, yes?"

Slowly he wrote "Béthune"—that one word I wanted. Oh, joy! I could have hugged the dear old thing! He had no idea that Béthune happened to be part of the front at the time! My luck appeared incredible! But he had written out my *sauf-conduit* right enough. It showed these names in black and white: "Amiens, Calais, Béthune." On my return to the hotel I communicated my good news to the *patron* and his wife; they grew quite sympathetically joyful over it.

None of us knew what difficulties lay before my enterprise. The *patron* helped to pack me up and off the next day. As before, my worldly belongings jangled from the saddle of the bicycle, and again he made that huge brown-paper parcel that could excel any yet seen suspended from ordinary cycles. Long ago I had failed to make any self-respecting Gladstone bag remain behind the saddle: I must therefore put up with that inevitable parcel. The *patron* tied on my parcel securely; and amid friendly waves from several hands I rode towards Paris.

Here I had to face another difficulty. My hair must be cut properly, according to military cut, yet without causing suspicion. Time helped

35

me. At St. Lazare Station I spent hours, presumably watching troops; really I was occupied in winning the confidence of two stalwart Scotch military police on duty at the station. Help I wanted; and they could either hinder or help. Three days that job required. Freckled Scottie at first thought I was a woman of loose morals; then thought, "I don't know what to make of you"; and finally thought, "She's a sporty kid. I'll help her." So one evening this military policeman handled very nervously—he hated cutting off my hair—a large pair of scissors.

"All right, little girl, I'll help you. But do you think it is worth it?" And he looked at my mouse-coloured hair, stretching to my waist.

"Cut away," I said.

And he cut.

Five minutes later I looked in the glass. Well, I won't say what I looked like! He had cut close to my head, in true outline of a British private.

"Now pass that razor along each side of my face."

He did so. Vainly I hoped that boyish bristles would sprout! They never sprouted!

Next day at dawn I started again for that big Paris station. In the half-light of early morn I saw people look twice at this stranger, who wheeled her cycle, and walked along in an odd outfit and with a white linen hat pulled over her eyes. Yes, I must have looked peculiar. Before that journey I had covered my face with some weakened Condy's fluid, producing, as I hoped, the requisite manly, bronzed complexion. When next I looked in the glass I only saw, however, that I had smirched my face rather than rubbed it, hence the result appeared as a very dirty face! At the station I managed to rub these Condy stains evenly over my face, then, emerging from the waiting-room, dear Scottie Military Policeman, on duty at St. Lazare, smuggled me into the train for Amiens!

My arrival in Amiens passed uninterrupted by any exciting incidents. Only a few hours later, however, I received a shock. After depositing my cycle in a shop, together with its parcel, I visited glorious Amiens Cathedral. As I passed through the Cathedral porch I noticed a *gendarme*; he eyed me critically. In return I only hugged those precious papers closer. He said nothing. I passed on. He followed. Then at the church door he paused, thrust in his head, beckoned.

"This Cathedral opens at two o'clock for visitors," he said.

Lies! I knew it. Really he had plotted my arrest, and I knew that too. *Gendarmes* are strangely superstitious, yet efficient, people; this

36

man feared to make arrests within Cathedral precincts. He lolled outside the door; perforce I must come out. No sooner had my foot left sanctified ground than this man tore off my hat with the exclamation:

"Your hair is short."

Recovering opportunely, I asked why it should not be short. Glaring suspiciously, the *gendarme* seized hold of my arm ready to marshal me off to the local police station. I protested. Just as he wished to fulfil the deed, out stepped a man from amongst the crowd of civilians, ready to champion my cause.

"Let me look at her passport."

I showed it.

"Why, that's her photo right enough. You can't arrest her. Let us look at her papers."

Pulling out my *sauf-conduits* once more, I showed them.

"They are quite in order. Let her go."

Very reluctantly the *gendarme* released my arm; and I took care to lose no time in getting my cycle and self on the high road from Amiens to the front. Before I went, I took a good look at the town that possesses one of the most gorgeous bits of architecture in the world.

Beautiful Amiens positively scintillated with shafts of golden sunlight; all the city was stirred with animation, and without any of those ghastly tokens of bloodshed that filled the fields only twenty miles away. The lighter side of warfare chiefly touched Amiens at this date; along its streets swift motors passed heavy lorries, picking their way among Red Cross cars; restaurants reverberated with laughter, the crowded rooms revealing French and English officers eating their meals to the sound of automatic pianos. Life here pulsed high with the full-blooded throb of healthy routine; twenty miles away, carnage had strewn the countryside with the disfigured forms of dead men. Between the town and this carnage there stretched a long white road that connected each with the other.

Along that white road I now cycled, with only 2s. 6d. in my pocket—either the front or risk of death in the effort. So often on these roads one comes across lone figures of refugees who, separated from the fugitive host, add poignancy to the sad picture by their very loneliness. One such I met. This woman tramped wearily along the road, after hours of steady plodding, *en route* for any convent ready to take in a forlorn refugee. Her home had passed to the Germans and she fled, with only one article of underclothing to her back, and a tiny

[handwritten marginalia: "Close call (but why?)"]

[handwritten marginalia: "(Amiens)"]

[handwritten marginalia: "1918 Battle of Amiens foreshadowing"]

child, who clung tightly to the bedraggled skirt. Glut of sorrow brings surfeit; perhaps that is why single figures of pain, seen in this great war, stamp on the mind of spectators indelible marks that vast crowds fail to make. Anyhow this homeless fugitive, knocking at a convent gate, and one other sight, made on my mind the deepest impression of what invasion really means.

That other sight was an entire family fleeing from its burning town. In the stifling carriage of a crowded train, open flew one of the doors, as the whistle cut shrilly through the air, and in tumbled a crate of squawking fowls, followed by a peasant, with his pots and pans, wife, bundles, and family. They all seemed mixed up indiscriminately. One fellow-passenger caught hold of the crate, and other passengers hauled in family, or belongings, according to what came first. And this *mêlée* represented one home on the move. "*Les sales Boches! Les sales Boches!*" no wonder the *pay sans* exclaimed.

Yet how kind towards each other French peasantry managed to be through all this horror. Forbearance and good temper reigned; and French politeness never ceased. Every one benefited by this spirit of friendliness. As I left Amiens, peasants came out to direct my cycle-rides.

"Go straight on; and you will arrive at Béthune."

So I rode straight on for 60 kilometres approximately; and these long rides through sweltering heat added to my unattractive appearance. Stains of Condy's fluid, looking like dirt, trickled down my face, and the heavy full-length blanket coat, worn for decency's sake, gave further discomfort. Truly, I looked *awful*! Discarding earlier in the journey all unnecessary clothing I had thus prepared for quick change into uniform; change to take place in some field at a moment's notice. Behind my cycle dangled in its parcel, cap, boots, uniform, and braces. It wouldn't do for soldiers to discover discarded petticoats in a field, thought I, hence I wore no petticoat. Essential underclothing I wore, of course, but without any non-essentials; outwardly there appeared only a green blanket coat, old boots, and a white cricketing cap pulled over my forehead. In that wonderful parcel, dangling from the back wheel of my cycle, I carried, with the uniform, the linen bag filled with methylated spirits and food. So I made for the firing-line.

Hours of uneventful riding passed, while I steadily covered the miles between Amiens and the front. Alas, at the time of writing that meant only a brief ride enough. Only what was beautiful marked the landscape for a long way ahead; excellently cultivated acres stretched

38

in undulating fields as far as eye could see. Once, in a while, peasants paused to look up from their field labour; and when I had hardly gone out of Amiens little children ran across the open road. Gradually civilians grew fewer; and at last none came my way.

Very few cars disturbed the ride; and only far distant sounded those steady boomings of cannon or cracks of *mitrailleuse*. Later, however, heavy firing became very audible and obviously not far away. Then came one or two unusual sights. A lonely grave was the first visible sign of war; innumerable hosts of golden corn-sentinels bowed their heads over this quiet grave of a British soldier who lay buried under the rich corn; ripe corn that stretched for miles in those fair fields of France. And one wondered could there be a more beautiful grave? Outlined by some friendly hand there it stood by the roadside. Visible, though embedded in thickcorn, it was noted, without doubt, by tramping thousands of dusty khaki lads, as they marched along that road for the sake of England's little hedgerows and those golden fields of France. No; it was not by accident that an English soldier lay buried in that spot. Nor without strangely different significance stood that broken pillar—dark against the blue sky and sunk deep in the blood-sprinkled soil of a distant hillock. There fought doggedly our khaki troops in one of the earliest battles; and the pillar marked the battlefield. Without beauty, grimly that pillar stood as a memorial of dogged courage, horror, tenacity, and arrested life; silent witness of Tragedy and Triumph combined in supreme sacrifice. It silently taught its lesson, and that lesson appeared grim enough.

Cycling farther I passed disused trenches; they must have been amongst those hastily dug earthpits, quickly made to stem our temporarily fugitive troops. Quite shallow, their narrowness minimized their usefulness, perhaps, though that remains a matter of opinion; anyhow, interlaced with wooden planks alternating with sandbags that lay in layers, as seen in pictures of sandbagged Amiens Cathedral, they had stood weather well and inclined the spectator to think that troops finished their construction at a later date or experienced less rush of retreat than England supposed.

Gunfire increased in reverberating noise; across the cornfields floated the sound of heavy booming interjected by loud maxim fire or nervous taps that came from *mitrailleuse*. All at once war, revealed up till now by graves and sound, took on itself human form. Silhouetted against the sky-line, a quickly galloping horseman trampled over the waving corn. Not much could I see, so far distant he rode. Suddenly:

39

"Arrêtez!"

Across my path there popped out two French sentinels. These men live usually within huts, established on the road, inhabiting small box-like sheds, lined often from ceiling to floor with interlaced straw; straw forms the mainstay of structure in these sentry-boxes. French sentinels suit their action to their command; before I could ride another twenty yards, the road lay blocked by a heavy French rifle held horizontally high above the head of the sentinel who had spoken. Holding out my papers I dismounted.

"Bien!"

This fearsome Frenchman, with his inky coloured beard, saluted, and I rode on! Meanwhile the distant figure of the galloping horseman approached nearer the road. Not many minutes later this khaki rider, as he proved to be, got alongside my cycle; and he did it intentionally, I realized that fact. He stared; and I knew that, as a woman, I certainly looked suspicious in this proximity to the zone of fire. Purposely I almost compelled the rider to go on ahead. Next, I passed water lorries, with their accompaniment of portable kitchens; those steaming iron-cauldrons slung behind horse and cart. Soldiers responsible for these carts took their ease, sprawling on the roadside. Not a few called after my retreating figure; I had long ago left any vestige of companionable womenfolk. No women had obtained permission to penetrate to this distance.

(cat calls)

After smilingly nodding to these soldiers, I came across a picturesque scene. Troops lay bivouacking among the corn. In batches British soldiers posed, unconsciously, making a picture that any artist would proudly have painted. Tiny clouds of grey smoke stole upwards slowly from British briar pipes as a soldier here and there lay alone, separated from a batch of companions. Taking their ease, lying in many different attitudes, these men dotted cornfields with splashes of khaki uniforms worn by living figures. Laughter rang through the air; nothing depresses these Tommies of ours. With jokes and a pull at their pipes, they were resting after presumably forced marches.

By this time the horseman endeavoured to get even again with my cycle. He came riding up. I spoke. He showed the usual astonishment at meeting with an English girl on this road.

"Where are you going?" He eyed me with suspicion; perhaps I might be a spy.

"Béthune," I replied.

"You won't get there on this road. Why, you are miles away. If you

40

go straight on, as you wish to do, you will certainly get to trenches—by falling straight into them. This road leads to Albert."

So I had been misdirected; and here I was on the wrong road.

"Well," I said, "night will set in before I get to Béthune, if I must go back. I think I'll go straight on."

My companion agreed; as he felt far from easy about my identity he silently established himself as my escort to Albert. From that moment his horse never failed to trot alongside my cycle.

"We are not at the front, surely," I said.

"Aren't we!" he replied.

Then we began to talk pretty freely about the front, and he said that our first line was outside Albert.

Nobody here at home realizes quite what "the front" signifies. To womenfolk that word implies one narrow line, called the fighting-line, with only such towns as fringe it. In reality the front embraces vast stretches of country, often miles away from the cannon-mouth, and without any scenes of excitement. "Front of the front," if I may thus describe that land which borders frontline trenches, offers monotony of existence hard to beat in any distant English village. Of course I do not describe the state of the front as experienced during a great push. In the daily life of ordinary days the front means deadly monotony to our English soldiers; and thus ennui gets periodically punctuated by intense excitement, together with horrible bloodshed. But this occurs only when "Yesterday there was great activity along the British front."

"Now where are we?" I inquired.

"The front, of course; and just getting into Albert."

I did not know it. Vast stretches of cornfield practically fringed the spot where he said the trenches began. Heavy gunfire kept up plenty of noise, it was true; but there was no cannon in sight, nor anything visible to denote front lines. Albert was so very much the front, however, as to be forbidden ground in those days to either war-correspondents or nurses.

"I'll come with you," said my youthful cavalier. He referred to Albert. Meanwhile we started to talk about his home life. "Here's my wife," he said, pulling from his pocket the usual postcard photo. To my surprise I saw the picture, not only of a woman, but of two little children with her. "They are mine," proudly announced this young man.

And he had only just said he was nineteen years of age! Nineteen and a married man with a family! Out of his pocket he pulled something else. A green apple!

"Have one?" And he held out a very green one.

"Have you others for yourself?" I asked, looking at this schoolboy-man.

For answer he dived once more and out came another equally green apple. And it was thus, soldier-boy and dirty-faced girl, both munching, we rode and pedalled into that "front of the front."

"Halt!"

I halted.

"Your papers."

Two stalwart Scotch laddies confronted me and one of them, lifting out his red head from a bucket of water, stared as I approached. Each appeared in his kilt only, his ablutions having occupied his time till I interrupted this solemn function. Full splendour of Scotch kilts requires complete uniform; anyone unacquainted with the Scotty robed only in shirt and kilt with head bared, fails to realize what a droll picture he looks! Quickly realizing that I had arrived, pierced the lines, in fact, of the 3rd Army, with its glorious names from the pick of Scotland's regiments, I looked around. Individuals represented Black Watch, Seaforths, Argyll and Sutherlands, etc. How splendid these men looked! Nearly all stood well over six feet high—broad, well-knit, magnificent: "The Contemptibles," mostly all dead men today.

"You must come before our officers," the red-headed sentry thus interrupted my reflections.

"Well, I can't go like this!"

I referred to my dirty face. It had been my intention, as already explained, to don khaki outside Béthune, when, the limit accomplished in female attire, I should thenceforth rely on disguise. Efforts at adequate preparation for quick change into man's clothes included that Condy stain, with which I had covered my face before I left Paris. My girlish colouring stood every chance of detection, hence the attempt to discolour my face. I rather wished also to appear conspicuously unattractive so long as necessity demanded that I should wear girl's clothing among regiments of men. Certainly I achieved this last object!

"You can wash your face here, if you like," said the sentry.

Meanwhile he fingered my bulky brown-paper parcel. I wished he would leave it alone; supposing there should protrude from it one corner of khaki! It seemed best speedily to divert his attention.

"Bored here?" I said, dipping my face into his bucket.

42

"Heavens, yes, here we live, eat, and sleep." And the place happened to be only a shed, put up by the roadside. "But how did *you* get here?" I had not time for answer; along came a cyclist scout. I first rubbed my face hard with the towel, sharing it with Scottie who handed it to me; and with steady rubbings I became only healthily brown.

"Now follow me."

I was conducted through Albert as far as the officers' quarters. As we passed along what had been the main street I noticed that here and there deep shell-holes scooped up the earth, leaving hollows of several feet deep; every shop appeared to be shuttered; occasionally shop-fronts showed window-breakages; and over all the guns boomed from ten minutes' distance away. Khaki figures dotted streets, singly or in groups, no women appeared in sight, and heavy wagons, piled with munitions, rolled through the streets.

(image and Albert (contrast w/other towns))

"Who are these? "I asked, nodding in the direction of some khaki figures who approached with tools in their hands.

"Oh, they're Engineers; probably they have been building up some damaged trench. Ready-to-go-anywhere men. Do duty on mine-laying as often as they build up trenches" replied my escort.

[Later I knew better what mine-laying involves.]
"Then how far from here do the trenches run?" I asked.

"It depends where you stand. Over yonder, do you see those cottage ruins?"

"Yes." In later days how well I was to know those ruins!

"Front-line trenches run just a few yards beyond them."

Well, I had certainly managed to get near the trenches! No information was more welcome at the moment.

As we walked, the deserted town became suddenly transformed from dismal neglect, though without ruined buildings, to a scene of abject ruin. Shell-holes pockmarked the streets, they went further, by creating gaps that made heavy walls to topple dangerously. Quite one hundred feet above the road there balanced betwixt earth and heaven the famous figure of the Virgin surmounting Albert Cathedral. Originally perpendicular, this statue, hit repeatedly by shells, gradually bent over the town till it stretched horizontally over the earth, balancing there, face downwards; it appeared in the act of casting down to that earth its Infant Jesus. Town folk said: "When the Virgin falls the war will end." The statue had not fallen then, although, bent by shell-fire, it looked perpetually ready to crash downwards. Each night the German guns made that once beautiful statue their target for the molten

43

lead of "Enemy Hate."

By the name of "Enemy Hate" our troops christened desultory nightly bombardments of the town. Sentinels posted round the ruins of the Cathedral kept off the unwary from falling masonry; these living men seemed further to intensify that picture of ruin around which they stood. Close by another war picture faced me. Jolly bands of Scotch troops, kilted, played football among the ruins in the gutter. They laughed Their genuine football, bouncing over fallen bricks, tumbled into shell-holes and along ripped-up pavement. Here the men followed it. Kilts fluttered, while players, shouting out in broadest Scotch, kept up their game. Through these scenes I arrived at the officers' door; passing first through an open courtyard.

good image

In an ordinary room, at a table, sat officers to the number of three or four, and amongst this number was an officer of the Black Watch Regiment. I produced my *sauf-conduit*.

"This is not Béthune," said one young officer, smiling broadly.

"No," I replied. "On my arrival I discovered my mistake. At Amiens I was told to keep straight on. To the best of my knowledge I did so and I arrived—here!"

Though in quite a gracious manner, the officer said I could not stay there!

"Of course," I said, "I understand that."

With the approach of evening, I had no wish to start out for Béthune, and with this reasonable objection I was given written permission to stay overnight in Albert.

"You will start tomorrow morning for Béthune?" said the officer.

"Yes," I replied; and at the time of speaking it was my intention to do as I said.

Everyone showed great surprise at my appearance in this part of the front; and it had already caused a sensation in the town. Owing to this fact there seemed every chance that detection would follow any attempt to transform myself into a khaki boy. Permission given for temporary rest in Albert, I was provided with an escort, in order to find sleeping accommodation in the town. No easy task to get any "shake down" in this "front of the front."

On my way through the town I attracted the attention of the soldiers, who, seeing a girl-cyclist, supposed that she must be a Frenchwoman with a special permit. *(because a Brit never would.?)*

"*Bon jaw!*" these cavalrymen kept shouting out.

And I replied:

"Don't '*bon jaw*' me; I'm English."

Not one of these men believed it; some said:

"She speaks English jolly well for a French girl, doesn't she?" And they evinced surprise that any French girl had gained sanction to get there at all.

That night I spent in a room, over a tavern, with windows barricaded, to keep out the draught from gaping shell-holes made in the glass. Below my room, the faint light only half lit the great barnlike tavern where troops, coming straight from the trenches, swarmed round the counter for drinks or a game of cards.

Having paid overnight for my lodging, I got up early. No one seemed to be on the premises; there was an air of desertion about the house. Before the battle of Loos—as this period happened to be—no one knew from hour to hour what might occur, and everyone held *(Biggest British offensive Sept 1915)* his life in his hand. I prowled about. No soldiers appeared in the long street, and there was I, trying vainly to find food. I got on my cycle, riding to the outskirts of the town. "Shell Cot"; these words, scrawled over the wall of a house, attracted my eye, they were written on the last house before the open country began. From Shell Cot, out popped a sentry; the name had evidently been scrawled by an Englishman who wanted to make his shell-visited sentry-box homy.

"Where are you going " asked the sentry.

"Exploring to find some breakfast; and as Albert does not appear ever to have breakfast I propose to see if there should be better luck in the next village." So far I had not yet spent that two and sixpence!

"Your *sauf-conduit* only applies to Albert; beyond this barrier you cannot go," said this troublesome sentry.

Another sentry appeared; and, seeing that I had attempted to leave Albert, this man showed suspicion.

"You'd better report to our officers, I think," he said, mentioning one of those individuals.

Whereupon I was again marshalled off to the authorities. We arrived; "authority" happened not yet to be fully dressed, and until I was interviewed I waited in a nice little sitting-room. Now it appeared that the officers had felt glad to see me; later one or two said so. Though an unlovely bit of femininity, as I certainly looked, with my Condy's fluid stained face and old coat, I spoke English; and out there they do so long for the sight of an Englishwoman's face. Once more I was presented. Briefly I said that I, not knowing my *sauf-conduit* forbade it, tried to get out of Albert, yet not in the direction of Béthune.

45

"Why?" queried X.

"Well, quite frankly, I was looking for some occupied house where I could buy my breakfast. I feel jolly hungry." And that was all the explanation I gave; as usual I briefly spoke the truth.

"Oh, I see!" X. laughed outright. "Come along then, and do have breakfast with me."

Though rather embarrassed at my uncouth appearance, I felt "jolly hungry." So I said:

"Thanks awfully."

Here, within yards of trenches, we sat down to breakfast, served by an orderly as nicely as at any English table! Breakfast consisted of porridge with salt, bacon and eggs, Dundee marmalade, and bread and butter. Being partly Scotch, I appreciated everything. Outside our room, rival guns thundered at each other! Inside it, these two strangers shared, as though quite at home, this thoroughly British meal. Certainly I looked like the typical vagabond. Corsets I had dropped; if obliged to get into uniform quickly I wanted no tell-tale clothing left about. I wore very little indeed! My one wrap, that full-length coat, covered multitudes of deficiencies! That coat I had purposely selected for the expedition; its covering satisfied rules of decency, whereas I could easily throw it into any passing hedge when I changed into uniform.

During breakfast I kept on that linen hat, pulled tightly over my forehead; fortunately X. refrained, with probably intentional tact, from suggesting that I should take off either hat or coat.

Long after this incident I said, "Didn't you see that I appeared only half dressed?" *(foreshadowing relationship)*

He answered: "Well, I thought you didn't seem to be wearing much."

In this brief visit I found my host very entertaining. Showing almost boyish confidence, he said how he longed for leave and that for twenty-seven weeks he had never left the trenches.

"Don't your people object to you going about like this?" he asked.

"They don't know," I very truthfully replied.

If that dear old Cathedral city in England had known of these escapades I think my highly respectable guardian, living there, might, perhaps, have had forty fits! As things were, I could get no money from England; and every one remained ignorant of my doings.

"But what are you doing out here?" continued X.

HC of war?

46

"Searching for newspaper copy," I replied. "I want to write about France as it is now."

"Oh, I see," replied my young host, seemingly satisfied with the explanation.

When breakfast was finished, he kindly saw me on the right road for Béthune.

"You go along there," he said, pointing out where I must ride for Béthune direction. We both laughed at my unwieldy parcel dangling behind that saddle. If only it had suddenly revealed its contents!

No one realizes better than myself that in writing this true account without shelter of *nom de plume,* I am incurring the risk of personal reputation. Knowing the risk I run, I accept its consequences. I write this book as a tribute rather in the light of discharging a debt do I set out this true story and write under my own name. Many readers will readily discredit this tale; and discredit rests on two distinct charges—facts queried and personal character assailed. To "take cover" under the cowardly shelter of a *nom de plume,* I do not feel inclined. Anyway I offer at least fair play by revealing as target my true identity. I come out into the open.

CHAPTER 4

On the March for the Trenches

Hardly had I started to pedal away from Albert than there occurred to my mind the notion that it might be foolish to leave this town at all. Why not accomplish my purpose here? In going to Béthune I might meet with bad luck; here anyhow I was on the spot for the trenches. These thoughts passed through my mind; I said to myself: "True, I do not know local passwords; on the other hand I am here, almost on the top of frontline trenches." Thinking thus, I scanned every passing soldier. "Too tall!" I said to myself. Never could I impersonate any Scotch troops.

As I walked along by my cycle, soldiers came up to speak, but at times their Scotch accent prevented conversation; I could not understand half a dozen words. No one tried to do me any harm. Rather I must make one exception; in efforts to tussle with me there occurred an unpleasant incident when I hit a man till, disliking kicks and the barking of his shins, he desisted, amid shouts from the comrades who disapproved his tactics! Throughout three and a half months spent at the front or near it, that one incident only broke the rules of British chivalry. Experience of those three months taught me that I deserved far worse luck !

All at once I spied a soldier whose height approximated to mine. Speaking a passing word, I jumped on my cycle to avoid the soldiers who were congregated where I stood. The little soldier followed. On escaping from the crowd I wished to speak alone with this small soldier, a native of Lancashire and unit of the Royal Engineers Regiment; I could gauge by speaking if he would harm any woman who put herself in his power, and if he possessed qualities I could utilize. Soon I had my chance. Watching where I should dismount this little sapper, as he proved to be, hurried up when he saw that I stopped the

48

cycle.

"I've been keeping an eye on yer," he said. "They'd have torn yer to pieces. I knew that, so I've followed yer up."

Pulling my cycle up a bank, I clambered over this grassy mound. Sapper and I sat down to talk. Very soon I realized that Sapper Dunn could be trusted he championed my cause at the outset. He possessed exactly, moreover, the very qualities required for a job which I anticipated he should undertake. He continued to act chivalrously in every way. Before five minutes passed Sapper Dunn knew exactly what I wished to do. Here in Albert I intended to "join up." Would Sapper Tom Dunn please help?

Before we could make plans it was necessary, however, that I should be temporarily concealed until the soldiers grew tired of hunting after my cycle. This fact Dunn carefully explained; and I grew slowly to realize then that the presence of a woman at the front possessed dangers other than death.] *really that naïve?*

"You don't realize what danger you are in," stated this middle-aged soldier.

We started fully to discuss plans for my immediate action. I thought it so strange that this uneducated soldier grasped my true character more quickly than Generals, later, proved able to do. In a very short time Sapper Dunn grew easy as regards probable espionage on my part; instinctively he realized I was English right enough in the same way as I knew instinctively that he was worthy of complete confidence.

"Yer already have yer uniform?" he asked.

"It forms this wonderful parcel," I replied, pointing to the bulky package.

He, experienced miner from Lancashire district, had joined the Buffs at the outset of war, though drafted later into the Royal Engineers.

"Now I'll get yer R.E. badge, name, and number."

He left me to procure these essentials, and on his return he handed over "The Buffs" badge as additional help in case of need.

"You stay where yer are while I scour round to see that the soldiers do not see yer," he said. "Let them think that yer have cycled away from Albert. I'll be back soon."

With that he departed while I sat there awaiting his return. I had not long to wait. He returned saying :

"I've said that yer are gone. Now take care not to appear again in

49

Albert as a girl; in khaki, as one of the troops, yer must come out in future. For the present yer'd better hide; give time for excitement to die down." Suiting his action to his words, Sapper Dunn climbed over the hedge, scanned the neighbourhood, and said :

"Now I see thoroughly the sort of girl yer are, I'll help yer. Yer no bad 'un. You're a lady. I followed yer to see what sort of gal yer was. I ain't no better than the rest. All the same I ain't agoin' to harm any gal. Yer're straight, that's what yer are. I can see that. So I'll help yer."

His words recalled to my mind, "There, little girl, I've done it for you," spoken by the Military Policeman while he cropped off my hair. In the same spirit those other men provided my outfit. Ten men eventually shared in this exploit. All gave me help owing to the fact that I behaved like one of their own naughty schoolgirls, and only later I realized how splendidly these men *had* behaved—rough soldiers, away from civilization, surrounded only by the coarsening influence of war! Yet no one harmed this fool of an English girl!

Not till I had returned to London's doubtful civilization did I hear the true meaning of "camp follower." While suspected by educated military men, I did not know what "camp follower" really meant; though I had often heard the term, I supposed it referred to wagons that carried provisions. Not once had our soldiers removed this idea. True, I kept concealed about my person a heavy military knife, ready for any emergency. No call came for its use.

Tom Dunn and I hunted for a fit hiding-place where I could remain. Stealthily making our way, we crossed some cabbage plantations, skirted the town, and arrived safely at those deserted cottages mentioned in connection with my arrival at Albert. In front lay the trenches, approached by a small cabbage plantation; at the rear Albert's statue of the Virgin balanced in mid-air, brooding over the place; and immediately below these cottages cellar dugouts offered ready shelter. Into one of these dugouts I plunged, pulling in that precious cycle.

"Now I must be off," said Tommy. "I know where yer are. As soon as I get off duty I'll report news."

Left alone, I started to disrobe, among the straw, preparing the transformation scene. In great agitation I very soon stopped—every inch of my body tickled and irritated. Ugh! creepy crawlies! creepy crawlies! Everywhere fleas jumped in all directions. Before an hour passed I was a complete mass of pink lumps; without exaggeration there jumped fleas in that dugout higher in number than the bristles of straws that covered the floor! No exaggeration! Whatever hap-

50

pened, I felt I must quit that dugout. Poking out my head, I looked for passing soldiers. None appeared in sight. "Must chance it!" I said. And out I got.

Quickly examining the row of cottages, I selected one as my temporary new headquarters. Three parts of the roof stood open to the sky; lying across the threshold, the shell-struck door was falling from its hinges, and inside the room, where I stood, there remained on the floor only a sodden mattress and a table. On wet days rain poured down on the mattress from the gaping roof. One significant thing I noticed: either soldiers had previously billeted here or occupants had fled without fully packing up. On the table there still stood a French wine-bottle and by its side lay a half-finished letter. A yard outside stretched the length of these one-roomed cottages, and here I found, attached to the wall, a cold-water tap, while on the ground lay a rusty jam cauldron. Beyond the yard began the local cabbage patch, and that practically fronted the German first-line trenches.

Later, I discovered that the row of cottages underwent regular bombardment nightly, when "Enemy Hate," sending its shells at the Cathedral target, hit holes in all the cottages which happened to lie across the direct line of fire. People had evacuated them. I started to move in. First, I pulled up the door into position, barricading it with boards; and then I took long draughts of cold water from that inviting tap. Foolish thing to do! In this way apparently I contracted septic poisoning, owing to poisoned water, which, after my return home, caused unfitness for work during a year and a half. My next job meant dragging out the mattress; and in so doing I discovered what a sodden load it had become.

Fortunately, I could make this moderate commotion without fear of detection; and thanks to a low wall which divided the yard from the cabbage plantation. Troops passed along to the trenches; they skirted my wall and yet they never saw me! To the red-rusted cauldron I devoted special attention; only a foot and a half in diameter, it was selected as a bath and a copper. How thankful I felt in securing that moderate comfort. Preparations looked complete when I had picked up some string, stretched this string from door to wall, and arranged for a speedy washing-day with the string as my clothesline. Only one bit of beauty remained to this ruined row of cottages; it stayed there through shell-fire and bomb—one tiny white rose clung to the side of the wall that divided trenches from homesteads! Poor little white rose; it looked so incongruous, so pathetic !

51

After I had completed these scanty preparations for my barracks, I waited for the little R.E. and his latest news. Evening drew on; and I began to fear that he had been detained. I waited and waited. Four hours probably passed in this way. Supposing Tommy never came? What should I do? What could be my next move? In Albert I should be recognized if I appeared as a girl, and as I knew nothing yet about local rules I could not enter the trenches as one of the troops.

Suddenly I heard steady footsteps advancing across the cabbage patch. In one moment my heart leaped with fear into my throat. If it should be a soldier ready to betray my hiding-place? Only a moment I waited; and the little figure of the R.E. came round the other side of the wall. How glad I felt at the sight of this little friend, standing only about five feet high! And I grew so hungry too. Perhaps he could buy food if I asked; and I still had quite a few pennies left from that half-crown.

"Hullo! Thank goodness!" Thus I greeted Tom Dunn. "I *am* glad you've arrived, it almost seemed that you would never appear again."

As soon as Tommy got under cover he plumped a Tommy's cooker on the mattress. In it steamed some excellent stew with gravy. My mouth watered. Together with the stew there appeared a large biscuit that resembled thin dog biscuits, and a hunch of bread.

"Here, I've brought yer this! It explains why I was so long."

Dear little fellow, he had waited at the regimental cookshop to gather up some food for this girl! Seating himself on the sodden mattress, Tommy waited while I ate my first rations.

Readers, do not suppose that our troops live on bully beef without variation of diet. No; often they eat excellently cooked food in good variety, though that depends whether the male regimental cooks happen to be experts at their job. Bully beef tastes not such a bad thing, either. Over here we eat bully beef, known as American corned beef, encased in blue tins. Between corned beef and bully beef there is no distinction. Through the army kitchens, our troops in the field often eat excellently made up dishes, soups and puddings. No, it is not always bully beef.

"Well, what news?" I asked, munching. "In that dugout I simply could not stay; fleas hopped in fighting battalions! This ruin suits all right, doesn't it?"

He agreed as to the suitability of my present quarters, though it would be unwise for me to stay there long; if he were missed by his comrades he might be followed here.

"It won't do for yer to turn out in daylight yet; wait till the excitement dies down. At present all the men are talking about that meeting with yer. Now they think that yer 'ave cycled miles away from Albert; I said that yer'd gone for food. So don't come out yet. Afterwards yer can fall into line with me as we march into the trenches for a night shift."

We agreed on the following plan. Not far distant from the cottage, some Royal Engineers were billeted, together with other units, at one of the largest buildings of the town, formerly a schoolhouse. Outside it, regiments lined up for the trenches, assembling first in the courtyard, where trestle seats were ranged under a big yew-tree. During the daytime the troops used this courtyard as an open-air smoking-room and place of recreation. Swarming through the courtyard at night, the troops gathered into line through the gate of the yard; and on these occasions I was to mix with the khaki crowd and march with these men under cover of the darkness. *Plan to join soldiers to trench*

One evening here sufficed to prove what constituted the chief danger spots. In front lay the "ditches"—best described by that term. Properly constructed trenches proved too lengthy a task for a tiny army, compelled, perhaps, to move out of its shelter at a moment's "push"; only later in the war real trenches at Albert succeeded the rough makeshifts that formed the foundations of the finer structures. In the "ditches" the regiments at Albert felt comparatively safe; the supreme danger was centred in the courtyard of the billet where Fritz regularly hailed his high explosives, contained in jam tins called trench mortars, Fritz's intent being to knock out units on their way to the front line of the trenches.

Variety of danger, in the form of "under fire," concentrated itself neither outside the billets nor, always, inside the trenches; it focused itself on that narrow stretch of no man's land, fronting the German trenches, where, approximately 400 yards from the German front line, I put in most of my time as a British soldier. I dispensed no military duty in trenches; as a soldier I divided the ten days and nights either alone in the open of no man's land, about 400 yards from the Boche front line, under simultaneous fire of shell, rifle, and shrapnel, falling into line outside the courtyard, already described, whence the regiment moved into the trenches, or within one of three dugouts appropriated at night for my own use; throughout several nights I slept alone, under fire, among the ruins, presumably within sight of Fritz, if he had only known!

With the utmost care Tommy gave instructions, as I ate my supper. Subsequently he went off, fearing lest his absence from quarters would create suspicion. He departed, saying:

"Yer won't be frightened here alone, will yer? After the shift I'll come back as soon as I can get away."

Thick darkness set in; and with it "Enemy Hate" raged in earnest. Lying on my mattress, I tried to sleep. It was difficult, though, to get forty winks! Crack! Crack! Crack! Stray rifle-shooting occurred between opposite trenches as soon as a head appeared above cover. Often flashlights failed to illumine targets, and stray shots wandered. "Pong!" (I discovered that I was under rifle-fire.) One of these shots found its way either inside my dug-out or perhaps struck that jam cauldron. I did not get up to look; without light I could not have found the mark! "Pong!" and then again one more "pong." Shots dropped about from rifle-fire, missing its aim. But this noise differed entirely from the heavy boom of "Enemy Hate," directed towards the bending statue.

Three distinct sounds accompany a shell on its travels. One boom signals its emission from the metal mouth. Noise follows, like low whines up windy chimneys, caused as the heavy shell beats back air as it travels through space, and last there occurs a "bang" with simultaneous crash of falling timber or masonry. That is what happens when "Enemy Hate" sends its shells. As bad luck would have it, Fate posted me for ten days and nights in the direct line of fire; shots whizzed by at the Cathedral target, travelling shells passed overhead every few minutes. None happened to fall absolutely on me; the ruins of the dugout showed where shells had already removed the roof.

Rifle-fire penetrated that night either the courtyard or where I slept; also shrapnel fell apparently that night on the cabbage-patch. Through the night, the intensity of the shelling increased till daybreak, dying down as morning approached. Often shrapnel kept direct line over my roof—as I could hear—without falling near where I lay; and on other occasions it just missed the Cathedral by falling nearer the cabbage patch. And it happened to be that cabbage-patch, also the brief stretch of no man's land, that formed the only intervening space between Boche trench and me!

By morning light I picked up the cap fallen from a shell, together with shrapnel bullets. And, later, I brought back to England that piece of brass, with its decimal figures, also its bullets. Fragments of falling shell made a noise, like hail, as they struck the cabbage leaves or stone-paved courtyard. In fact, there is the sound of several different noises in the progress of one shell; other sounds accompany rifle-fire.

About two o'clock I looked across to the firing-line through limitless black density of starless sky, so pitch the sky appeared that night. As I watched, complete black gave place to sudden illumination, through brightly-coloured star-shells that threw up red lights, varied by purple stars. These stars, poised momentarily in mid-air, fell again with a stream of brilliance, lighting the sky for direct rifle-fire. In this way killing takes place artistically!

Later I looked again. No star-shells went up. Instead, pitch darkness covered the sky; except away to the right. Here how wonderful it looked. Ripped into gaping wounds, this smooth inky sky revealed wide splashes of blood-red—resembling, indeed, red gaps, like open wounds, made by some gigantic sword, in the black body of night. So it was that shells, igniting hayricks, set up such wondrous sky-effects. White floods of light turned night into day occasionally; and then shots rang out from enemies spying each other across opposite parapets; or little balls of fire, sent up by those star-shells, revealed solitary soldiers stationed in either trench. "Stand to!" In the trenches at night frequently this order signalled preparedness for sudden German attack; bayonets, glinting motionless for hours together below our parapet, marked khaki reception for the German "rush the trenches."

In the year 1915 trench warfare was still in its infancy; opposing forces struggled with the savagery of brutes without the aid of science as asset that tends towards polished cruelty by scientific methods; these followed later. "Barbarians!" retort critics, judging German methods. Cammaerts, the Belgian poet, aptly points out repeatedly that *barbate,* with its real significance of primitive savagery engaging war on primitive lines, ill suits, as criticism, the German system of warfare as developed in its later stages. "Barbarism" perhaps suited the style of warfare as practised on the Western front in its earliest days; at later stages, contributions of civilized genius to the arena of battle provided polished culture to death-dealing, while converting that human dealer from the majesty of the savage to the automatic wielder of complicated instruments of torture.

In 1915 German and English frequently faced each other; each experienced the Law of War, the sporting chance, when time and circumstance decide the issue. Informality marked trench-warfare at this date; once in the trenches Royal Engineers, for example, experienced no undue difficulty with discipline, as discipline, from officers. The C.O.'s quietly passed along the trench, surveying work generally;

as long as each unit worked, officers excited no particular notice nor required any. As regards mine-laying on a night shift; how do you lay a mine? Maybe readers ask that question.

At dawn the relief party takes the trenches; falling informally into line, each man slips gently down the side of the ditch, passing along to his allotted point. Fritz often pots with jam tins all the way to the trench! Few mines sink deeper than one hundred feet; into their mine two R.E. units descend, by ladder, or along cuts on the clay wall. Necessarily two men descend together; one to prepare the fuse while "mate" lays the mine. I declined, after thought, the duty of setting light to the fuse, preferring that "murder" should not rest on my conscience; I happened not to be to a *bona fide* soldier; agreeing with Tommy, as I did not anticipate betrayal at the time, that I should be the one to prepare the fuse, when it fell to his lot to set the match if no officer performed that duty.

Fritz bores from the opposite trench; and the entire art of mining rests in anticipating the moment when Fritz's engineering achieves the junction between both mines and inevitable explosion to one. Lay the fuse, let the officer fire it; and get out—maybe to face an adventurous Boche creeping up, with his glinting bayonet, under shadow of the parapet! Tommy, taking a breather, seated close to a half-laid mine, arrived at the top of the mine one night just in time to frighten away a Fritz who crept warily to what appeared as one of our unsentinelled mine-heads! Tap! tap! tap! tap! tap! Fritz mining away very close at hand; he's boring his tunnel! Quite gentle little taps that no miner fails to take as warning. They mean instantaneous death to one or other of the opposing miners. So often one of those signal taps disturbed the quiet nights on the front that brought a solemn splendour all their own; these nights beautify the landscape by the very weapons that are committing destruction at the moment they charm.

On my first night near the trenches I made enough discoveries to enliven the whole night through. Before my little R.E. reappeared I had arranged, though there could be little done, to make this ruin as homelike as possible. Getting up from my wet mattress, which had already given the cold that it forewarned, I tried to make a gipsy fire within the roofless part of the place. No, the fire refused to go; perhaps the sticks were damp. I abandoned that idea. Then I dragged the rusty cauldron, only six inches deep, under the tap, and I again dragged it, filled this time with water, to my mattress. In the wonderful linen bag I had carefully put soap, and I now prepared to have a bath in the rust-

56

THE AUTHOR ON LAND ARMY WORK

encrusted cauldron. Intensely thankful I felt at the prospect of a bath; and I did really have one in this circular diminutive basin.

No sooner had I soaped myself thoroughly than—sounds! Yes, unmistakable footfalls through the cabbage plot. For once I felt sick with horrible fear. Caught like a rat in a trap, I could not escape. Tugging that blanket coat round myself, I cowered down. Perhaps it might be the little R.E.? I waited. The footfalls made straight for the courtyard; and I scarcely breathed. Suddenly a Frenchman tiptoed amongst the ruins, evidently searching. For what I did not know! So far, he had not got up to my shelter; he peered into the neighbouring corners. He looked up. He caught sight of me. He approached. I quailed. Then he said, "*N'ayez pas peur, ma fille*," and went by the way he came. *["don't be afraid, my girl"]*

As I watched his retreating figure, I felt astonished that he showed no surprise at discovering an English girl amongst the ruins! Fortunately I had not spoken; perhaps he surmised that I was French. Anyhow, it was extraordinary to find any girl in such surroundings. Later, I understood better. In five minutes he was back again with steaming coffee held out for me to drink; evidently I was to understand that he felt no unfriendliness nor intended to do harm of any kind. In fact, he felt this way: "Least said the better"—for he was a looter! *[looter (character?)]*

Not long after this incident Tommy came. I related what had happened.

"Oh, Frenchy evidently wished to loot. Here he found yer. He feared yer might tell."

Anyhow I saw no more of the visitor, and he had done only a kindly action towards me. On the other hand, I felt that I might be detected here at any hour of the day; it seemed unwise to stay longer than appeared strictly necessary in the cottage.

Sir Galahad, as the little R.E. deserves to be called, came whenever he could get away. As I depended on him entirely for food, I was forced, when he could not come, to exist for twenty-four hours on water and a piece of bread! Rain trickled into my room, in certain corners of it, while steady channels came splashing down where roofless corners offered no protection; already my throat had become scarlet with rheumatism and I felt ill through hunger. Tommy Dunn did his utmost for my welfare; but he could not help the weather! If I liked, I could cycle away, dressed in girl's clothes, as far as Béthune, provided I left Albert. To do this I must abandon my project so long as I could walk I determined to stick on here.

Hours passed in complete loneliness. I could not yet go to the trenches in daylight; I must wait here. So I decided to have a washing-day. In that becrusted cauldron I had my first washing-day within hail of the trenches. Scrubbing hard with my bit of soap, I then hung up the clothes on the line just below the wall; one slender bit of string I had for a line. There within sight of the trenches, only a few yards from them, an English girl hung up her washing to dry! How strange it appeared, this mixture of domesticity and war!

After drying my clothes in the hot sun, while I sat wrapped only in my coat, I experimented with my uniform. In those long hours, when rifle-fire kept off solitude, I learnt by very much practice how to put on puttees so that they do *not* slip about one's ankles. Also a padding of cotton wool requires careful adjustment when it is used as padding of the human figure. It all took time. In my cap I stuck the R.E. badge; after which, facing the worst difficulties last, I proceeded to thin myself. Those folds of bandaging, generally in use for hospital purposes, I pulled taut round my body, placing layers of cotton wool between the folds; and I completed the change, as at the Paris hotel, by fixing a suspended sack round the curve of my back. Really I looked like that advertisement picture of a man enveloped in pneumatic tyres! Last came the uniform; I wore it over a man's striped shirt.

This *toilette* occasionally stopped short, if passing aeroplanes attracted my attention. Going outside into the yard I saw, whirring only a few feet from earth, hostile Taube planes, two or three, and often only one, prowling immediately above our trenches; so close came these planes that rifle-shots rang out, attempts to hit with shots from handy riflemen. I was attracted by the difference between the rival aeroplanes, as regards appearances. The German Taube looks heavy, as compared with the aerial British machines, its build seems solider, shorter, and more durable. The wings of the Taube appear as solid wood, compared with the effect given by English craft, as though our machines lightly skimmed through the air.

Dressing became easier with practice. I grew to fear far less that I should be detected. In Tommy's absence I used to venture out; and I watched troops, marching with steady step, often only twenty-five men together. They whistled the "*Marseillaise*" or a comic song. And there strode a young officer, in Glengarry cap. He stepped out as leader and gave words of command. Just on the other side of my wall, these troops passed along. Shrilly rang out the whistling chorus, breaking from time to time into words, as the steady tramp passed from the streets, along the cabbage patch, and straight for the front-line trench.

(How *gradually* life merges into death!) So I thought when I watched those men. It appeared, when those passing companies pierced the distance along that road, as though that road formed the anteroom opening direct on to the corridor of death. And that corridor was formed by the long line of serpentine trench.

On occasions when I mingled, by daylight, with other soldiers, I took care that Tommy stayed near at hand. "Goodnight," said passers-by.

"Goodnight," Tommy replied. And I purposely remained silent. Neither did I venture among civilians; always I feared betrayal through my voice. So I continued to exist on scraps, both food as well as conversation !

For several days I spent my time between my own private "barracks"—that is, alone in those shell-swept ruins—and with the troops. Since my arrival I had shifted my dugout lest stray looters should discover that I kept away, whenever I went into the town, from the main body of the men. Always I welcomed the privacy of my "barracks"; there I could get free from regimentals and loosen those tight bands that encircled my body. I loosened those bandages as often as possible!

One night Tommy called for me. Coming under cover of the cottage, he said: "Tonight I go on night shift, and yer can come, too; meantime we will wait here till it is dark. After dark we will creep along to the courtyard, mingle with the crowd, and line up when they do."

I agreed, feeling delighted with the arrangement. We rehearsed what I must do.

"You remember exactly what to do."

"Yes," I said.

And some hours later we started.

"Follow me." I did as I was told. "Now come along quietly."

We got out to the road, passed remnants of ruined wall, zig-zagging in uneven shapes, and brickwork loomed dark through the night.

"We are just by the barracks," said Tommy, speaking in a low whisper. "Those ruined walls face it. Ready?"

"Yes," I whispered, and my heart throbbed somewhere in the middle of my throat.

"You remember your regimental number and name?" he asked.

"Yes," I replied quickly.

Suddenly a white light flooded the courtyard, and the door flew open. Out streamed khaki figures. One man reeled, his form silhouetted against the sky. He was drunk; and I learnt that drunken men do sometimes march to their possible death. Hastily moving amongst his men the N.C.O. prepared his line.

"Now then."

Hearing the words of command I got away from the wall, and mingled with the moving throng.

"March! Left, right, left, right, left, right."

And I?

Chapter 5

Arrest

Fainting fits started to bring disgrace on the King's uniform, after ten days and nights spent under almost incessant fire, through havoc of rheumatism, from exposure and without regular rations, together with the after-effects of two months spent previously in different parts of the front or war zone.

I thought, "If I am knocked out by Fritz in the trenches, or only temporarily unconscious through faintness, there is no shadow of doubt that my sex will become known; and what will happen at that rate to my little army of khaki accomplices? They'll get detected without doubt, if I am rendered unconscious. One's captain can't very well tell a girl sapper that her services are no longer required in His Majesty's Forces. No reason on earth why he should be prevented from saying it, or seeing that it is said, to each of my little army of ten khaki men. Dear me, *if* authorities made a discovery of the full total involved, I'd be responsible for bringing my little army to irretrievable disgrace. Instant steps shall be taken."

In some such strain I argued. "No leader forfeits his units; without hesitation every British officer stands in the breach for the purpose of saving his men from betrayal into the enemy's hands. H'm! If then I take a step that risks surrender so far as I am concerned, shall I be a coward? I suppose not. I suppose I'd better take that step." In my mind I hastily gripped the immediate situation. All papers in my pockets likely to throw light on how I arrived, I burned.

In numbering off my little regiment, absent and present, these units formed it. Courier, first of my army, gleaned while I was in Paris, secret importer of my cycle across the Channel—if I remember rightly, through his kind services my cycle landed in France; news of a war-correspondent nature he would convey by hand to a certain London

[handwritten marginal note: Chivalrous Justification]

63

newspaper. Ex-Horse Guardsman, this man, over 6 ft., ready to re-enlist, rejected as "far too old." A certain renowned Whitehall officer, with whom I was acquainted long before I left England, sent out two boxes of chocolates; seated in the forest under distant fire I remembered that I had munched those chocolates with relish. I realized that he would be dragged into the unpleasant limelight! Two donors of my uniform, those khaki laddies, men of the Leicestershire Regiment, whom I have described at length; they fell into my little account. Poor old *maire,* who provided *sauf-conduit* for Béthune, unconscious that it happened to be the front! My Military Policeman, who, at Gare St. Lazare, cut my hair and subsequently helped my departure! Scotch officers, Black Watch, etc., blissfully unconscious that I remained anywhere near Albert! Tommy, my accomplice, and regimental comrade throughout. And one extremely highly placed staff officer in the field; he might be dragged into this business! The latter remained entirely ignorant that I happened to be at the front, far less that I belonged to His Majesty's Forces!

I decided exactly what to do. My plans had to be altered; it had been my intention to gather leisurely any news at Albert as war-correspondent, redonning my long green coat, leave Albert with my *sauf-conduit* and appear as a soldier in khaki at the London newspaper office.

"Tommy," I said, "you have my permission to let Sergeant into the secret, say that there happens to be a girl in the ranks. Tell Sergeant yourself."

I rehearsed. "Now, of course, I trust that you keep this secret, sergeant. In revealing my identity, I do not wish to leave the regiment; we only include you in the secret in order to safeguard my accomplices in case I get 'knocked out' or ill. No reflection rests on you through your knowledge of my identity; in case of unconsciousness on my part, you see to it that one of the regiment finds me. Let a newcomer on the scene be the one to discover my identity. In this way all concerned get clear of any hand in this job."

As regards the trenches, I felt no particular fear. In the event of the mine exploding when Tommy and I happened to be at work there would be few remains to identify; also I had planned against a post-death charge of espionage. I had arranged to leave both my passport and will outside the mouth of the mine. In case I should be blown up, my khaki comrades would discover that passport with its photo, together with the will enclosed in it. One day I had made my will. It was done while I was resting in no man's land. In arranging to divulge my identity I chose a cottage in the town for the sergeant to hear the tale. By appointment Sergeant X., looking pleasant, without N.C. manner, arrived on the scene. I came right out, boldly in uniform, to meet him.

"At once I will set your mind at rest on one score, sergeant," I said. "I am no spy; here is my passport. By birth I am English, but of Scotch and Irish descent." Here I produced the passport with its photo.

He seemed to believe everything; and he maintained that affable manner. He said very little; only he asked me one or two questions. After several minutes he went, agreeing to come another time.

Both men went out together. Later Tommy returned; he only knew that the sergeant intended to call on the morrow. Before he went, the sergeant had agreed entirely with my project. After Tommy had gone I remained alone, without light, for several hours in my temporary refuge; I watched the dusk deepening into night. Shortly after thick darkness had set in, I heard heavy footfalls, and they came towards my new abode. No walls lay in ruins here, in the centre of the town; neither had this place any gaping opening instead of a door. All at once the door flew wide open; and in marched three men. I noticed the sergeant closing the door. He stood on duty, as he posted himself near it. He came as escort for an arrest —and *I* was the person to be placed under arrest! In a tiny room that led from the front room, I watched the arrival of these three khaki figures. Each held a flashlight; and three flashlights played white light round the outer room.

"Oh, she's gone!" said one of the men.

Again they looked. On the other side of the half-open door I stood, absolutely motionless. These men failed to look round the door. I remained securely sheltered.

"Oh yes, she's gone right enough. Come along!"

And the three marched out. Just as they pulled the outer door I called out:

"Here, boys, it is all right; I am here right enough." And I stepped out into the glare of the flashlights, turned full in my direction.

"We arrest you in the King's name."

"Oh, I see," I said. "Perhaps you would like to look at my passport. Here it is. And I pulled out passports with *sauf-conduits* included. "Before this arrest takes place I wish to make it clear that I am not a spy. I am an English girl." One man turned his light on my papers, glanced at me, and seemed uncertain what to think.

65

"And you," I said, turning to the sergeant, who looked proud of himself. "You are the biggest blackguard I have ever met. If I *were* really a man I'd knock you down here and now."

Standing stiffly to attention, with his rifle tightly clasped, he replied;

"I am a British soldier. I am a soldier of the King." It was not so much the arrest that caused my indignation—it was the *way* he betrayed me. Doubtless he felt, however, that he was fulfilling his duty; anyhow, of the dead speak no ill, and he was killed only a few days later. In the days to follow, it solaced my mind to remember that I was never captured; had I *not* stepped into the outer room, they would have hunted in vain. They found my place of abode, turned searchlights on it, and *then* failed to see me!

I was placed under arrest, and taken through the darkness to headquarters. On each side I had a guard; a third man walked ahead. Talking as we went along, I learnt that I must go before the Colonel and other officers, billeted in one of the large Albert houses. Luckily darkness sheltered this humiliating little procession from observation. For that shelter I felt glad. If passing soldiers had stared, I should have looked so foolish; as it was, the quartet arrived at its destination without anyone knowing that it had passed through the streets. Just outside headquarters there sat one, as though at the receipt of custom, presiding over a little table. Before this personage I was arraigned. Here I underwent my first cross-examination. With few questions asked I was passed over to the Colonel. He happened to be in the mess-room with several other officers. Escort walked close at my heels. Together with several kilted officers interested in this episode, the Colonel awaited my arrival; meanwhile, as I passed through the door, escort stood on guard at fixed attention till, at the Colonel's orders, he ceased to be on duty.

My manner of coming into the Colonel's presence proved disarming in its effect, I must say. There I stood and I burst out laughing! Really I could not help it! So utterly ludicrous appeared this betrousered little female, marshalled solemnly by three soldiers, and deposited before twenty embarrassed men. On arrival I heard:

"Oh-O-O-! (groan) it is a woman. Certainly we shall never get even with a woman, if she wishes to deceive us."

News at the front spreads quickly; officers heard how there had been brought in a girl-prisoner. As I talked to the Colonel, the door kept opening to admit young officers. They felt anxious to hear the news; and all round the room chairs filled up with newcomers. Through the haze of tobacco-smoke I looked across a dining-room table, where stood whisky and glasses, and I glanced at this phalanx of kilted young officers. Men bent forward, anxious to hear how I had done it. In five minutes I had disarmed suspicion regarding whether I was a spy. Quite briefly I related exactly what had happened, explaining how I arrived in Albert and that I only stayed in the town on second thoughts. Attentive khaki figures bent forward, putting occasional questions, as they listened to what sounded an incredible tale. All at once the door flew open with a swing; in came a young officer, who having seen me last *en route* for Béthune about two weeks ago, exclaimed breathlessly:

"Good Lord, Miss Lawrence, whatever *is* the matter?"

Laughing, I answered:

"Nothing. Here I am. That's all. I have arrived here after staying two weeks in Albert."

Roars of laughter followed this announcement. Every one present laughed.

"What, you've been here ten days?" exclaimed the astonished officer.

"Yes, since I last saw you."

Laughter followed once more.

My arrest turned into rather a pleasant social evening; the Colonel, being my host and judge, talked "London" with me, and he and I discovered mutual acquaintances. However, these facts brought with them another difficulty. They caused additional embarrassment to headquarters. What could be done with me? Where could I sleep?

"You see," said the perplexed Colonel, "I do not know what to do with you! Here we have no accommodation for ladies. What on earth to do with you I do not know."

Seated at the table I lapsed into feminine attitudes, despite my little khaki uniform, concealment being no longer necessary.

"Anyhow you have caused excitement at the front," exclaimed one officer. "This episode will get talked about all along the line."

And one or two officers, filling their glasses from the decanter, sat nearer the table, while they chuckled with amusement.

It must have been eleven o'clock when the Colonel, having given orders previously, lighted a candle, and escorted me to my bedroom. Holding aloft this candle, he led the way to another small sitting-room, where the couch, made up as temporary bed, stood near the piano, and looked comfortable after what I had experienced lately.

"This is the best we can do, I am afraid," said the Colonel. "I'm locking the door for your own sake. Goodnight."

He departed, locking the outer door as he went; and I was left in supreme command of a little suite that included bathroom and lavatory. Phase one of my arrest showed rough handling of a possible spy by private soldiers; and the next phase revealed a group of embarrassed officers interviewing a young woman who appeared decidedly out of harmony with the official surroundings. Far from the last phase this proved to be. While undressing, laughter drifted into my room. It came from that group of officers; they were talking over their odd "prisoner of war."

Throughout the night I slept soundly, feeling thankful I need anticipate neither bombs nor betrayal. On the following morning, breakfast was brought in: eggs and bacon with tea and bread and butter. Later two visitors called; the first, being the Colonel, inquired had I slept well, and my second visitor, a young officer, asked for whatever papers I had in my possession. Accompanied by one of the Secret Intelligence Department, this officer, provided with orders to get everything, obviously disliked the job of reading my private correspondence. It had entered my mind that capture involved search, hence to safeguard my little army of ten I had wilfully destroyed papers likely to lead to their identification. When asked concerning the well-known officer in Whitehall who had sent out two boxes of chocolates, I owned to the chocolates! Whatever remained in the pockets of my khaki tunic supplied no better information of national use than that Major So-and-so had despatched two boxes of chocolates! How disappointing for my judges! Throughout our brief meetings the young officer behaved with the utmost courtesy; evidently he hated the whole business that attended the arrest of a girl.

After the search party had gone, I remained alone till after lunch. As my window overlooked the grounds, the Colonel experienced difficulty in preventing soldiers from talking through the window. Standing at a French window, he kept order by significant glances opposite. Whenever soldiers attempted to cross over, he exchanged snatches of conversation with the prisoner, who, perched on a window-sill, talked volubly from the sitting-room! So far I remained in khaki; no other clothes could be found.

And I heard later that the Colonel felt so embarrassed at the situation that he said: "Anyhow, whatever you do, take her away from here!

I don't know what to do with her."

On the afternoon that followed my arrest two officers, both attached to the Secret Intelligence Corps, one being a staff officer, arrived in my room.

"We have come to take you away," explained one.

And I was informed that I was to go where I could be provided with more suitable accommodation. The journey would take some time. Walking away from the sitting-room one of them said:

"How can we get her there?" looking perplexed.

"Have you an extra mount?" I asked as they stood beside their horses.

"We'll see what we can do," replied the staff officer; and his man went off to find a horse. Conversation between staff officer and me began on these lines :

"You've got yourself into a pretty pickle, haven't you?"

"Oh, I'm all right," I replied. "What a fuss you fellows make about it."

"But what will they say at home?" he asked.

Meanwhile along came my horse; and a fine mare she looked, too. Scrambling into the saddle I started off, as prisoner of war, between two guards. Only when at a brisk trot I realized how fearfully difficult horseback becomes when the rider happens to be a buxom girl, clad in male uniform, riding astride a man's saddle. I felt a keen wish for those discarded bandages; as it was I felt disgustingly immodest, in uncorseted "looseness," astride this mare. Owing to this feeling I made no attempt to ride properly; purposely I hunched up my body, reducing jolts. In my estimation there can be nothing immodest in the appearance of a woman dressed in male attire.

Strange I must have looked, indeed, riding between two guards, leaving Albert for the open country roads. Several miles we had covered, laughingly discussing my escapade, while my companions, feeling convinced that I was no spy, grew solicitous concerning my welfare. Suddenly the bay mare reared; taking exception to a passing haycart, she showed pretty spirit by repeated efforts to unseat her rider! Docile animals rank with extinct volcanoes, fit for calm contemplation rather than as objects of practical utility!

Not one of these beasts proved my mare; resembling the erratic temperament of womanhood, in feeling uncertain from moment *eye roll* to moment what her feminine unruly spirit might next inspire she danced on this occasion almost perpendicular with the sky! She and

I engaged in quite a heated argument; we queried as to whether she should first unseat her rider, or whether I should curb the fine beast without tugging on that finely-tempered mouth! Together we came to agreement; and then I found time to notice how pale one of the escort had grown in the process of this incident.

"Why don't you marry?" one inquired. At this date I forget what reply I made; nor whether I asked the association between curbing a horse and marriage. Shortly afterwards I remember that we passed gangs of Labour units, working on the roads, and as these men looked up one of my guard tried to shelter his young prisoner by riding just in front.

Eventually we stopped at a French hamlet; here, prepared for our arrival, a French officer came forward, a member of the Secret Intelligence Corps, with information as to where I could be lodged. I was conducted into the general room of a large farm, where the proprietress, busying herself by ladling out milk, stopped work to show me into a clean, sparsely furnished bedroom. When I had drunk some milk, I was told, as another member appeared from the S.I. Corps, that I was to lodge here. This new arrival dogged my footsteps. Dressed in civilian clothes he never lost sight of his charge for two seconds, following me into the bedroom.

Then the staff officer abruptly suggested that he should cease worrying me by unnecessary questions. "Don't bother the girl like that," he said. In this farm I had passed several hours when, as the next move, I was taken to the guard-room, not far from the farm, where several soldiers had assembled. Hastily passing through the throng, there stepped forward a renowned General who, glancing in my direction, said:

"Find some decent clothes for her; get her away from here."

Khaki seemed to be decent, I thought, in time of war; however, I fear that I said to the august personage—General Rawlinson, I believe—quite on the spur of the moment:

"Right O!"

No other clothes were conveyed to me; indeed, troops supplied khaki, but not skirts! So I went about, though under arrest, as a khaki-clad little soldier.

"You're not to stay here."

I found myself confronted by six feet of burly good-nature dressed, if I rightly remember, in civilian clothes. Apparently this latest arrival belonged to Scotland Yard or S.I. Corps; and it was into his charge that I must pass temporarily. Before evening set in, he drove me away in a car, drove miles through the country to an unknown destination. Those few weeks of semi-starvation and damp had had their effect, and fainting fits and sickness made constant cross-examination highly unsatisfactory for both parties. On this motor ride I felt horribly ill; and showed it.

"I feel sorry for you; why ever did you do it?" inquired this officer.

After that long ride we arrived at Senlis, so they said, if I rightly remember, though this place was not the Senlis that I had recently visited. Getting out of the car I was taken to the officers' mess, where, my companion going in to dine, I was put in the adjoining room to have my dinner. Later on cross-examination took place for about the sixth time already; unhappily my sense of humour was aroused, thanks to the appearance of my latest judge, whose normal occupation in war-time was to examine *German* prisoners! As I happened to be neither German nor spy, he proved rather unsuitable for examining an English girl. Anyone neither spy nor German appeared utterly to baffle his powers.

He arrived, on this special mission of examination, by car. I watched his arrival. Surrounded by two or three other officers, this little judge, standing perhaps less than five feet high, emerged from his car, muffled up to his ears, though it was hot midsummer, begoggled, noticeable. He advanced across the courtyard, deeply engrossed in conversation. Arrived in the mess-room, he sat down near the shaded lamp at a writing-table; and made up his mind, as it soon appeared, that I intended only to tell lies. In point of fact I followed my usual procedure; I told the truth. As no one could give information other than I myself, I should have thought that the little man might have found it politic, apart from all else, to pick his way carefully, unless he found I answered unworthily. Though subjected to the most searching cross-examination, I told the simple truth and nothing beyond it.

"Impossible! Nonsense! Incredible!" These exclamations scarcely helped forward the job of extracting the truth. At first I felt furious; then I laughed outright, and he felt distinctly annoyed. At the part of my story when Senlis came into the narrative, I certainly appeared to speak contrary to the facts of the case; not knowing that there are two Senlis in France I described one town while he kept in mind the other. In particular I described the condition of Senlis railway station; this proved my falsehoods, so he thought. We went on. We both contradicted each other. We got no "forrader." I laughed outright at certain remarks that my cross-examiner saw fit to make. Further irritated by this flagrant lack of respect on the part of the spy, my judge neither made headway in his case nor gave any satisfaction to the assembled officers, who depended on his skill alone for the revelation of my true identity.

CHAPTER 6

Tried at Third Army Headquarters

Cross-Examined by one of the best known men in the British Army I failed completely, through sheer truthfulness, to throw light or clarify the case in his estimation. This funny little man, striking terror in the hearts of German spies, evoked only laughter from an ordinary English girl. So I was sent on to the headquarters of the Third Army; there to be re-examined. Though feeling horribly sick, I had to jolt once more over shell-scarped roads which, when one feels ill, make motor-rides as uncomfortable as they can be. Many miles intervened between my last destination and the place known as Divisional head-quarters.

On arrival I was taken to the guard-room. In the dark I was conducted by an N.C.O. to my sleeping-room, where, stepping over sleepless forms, I arrived in a tiny room that adjoined the guardroom. In the filthiest of sheets, on an unmade bed, I had to sleep, with eight men lying asleep outside my door. No woman was allowed to speak to me on any pretext whatever; wholly at the mercy of guard-room occupants I was left for three nights.

To the credit of English privates, I found them as chivalrous as the soldiers who had already befriended me. Those men in the guard-room, ashamed presumably of their officer's action, endeavoured later to make my imprisonment in their midst as little irksome as possible.

Unique undertakings are removed from ordinary standards of judgment owing to their unique character; hence it appears to my mind as no argument for the defence of placing me with men that I had not shrunk from joining the ranks as a man. Leaders form their own plans; they become solely responsible for their own campaigns. When organizing the exploit, I allowed at the same moment for methods to suit the exceptional undertaking.

Every man of my own special army contributed exactly his share in the furtherance of the exploit; and I saw to it that I included only picked men, selected for their fitness through qualities of personality as truly as they appeared suited also through fortuity of circumstances. I knew exactly what to expect from each unit; ultimately the betrayal owed itself to the fact that circumstances themselves included one agent in this exploit whom I alone never picked as one of my chosen number.

On leaving England I brought into France not one written line of outside influence towards the accomplishment of this exploit. Every item of my plans I built up as I went along, depending on instantaneous variation of plan to suit alterations made by any passing moment. As regards time, six weeks cover the period of organization; within that time I picked my forces, concentrated their strength and individual duties, set in motion simultaneously the complete organized body of collected units. Diversity of gifts, but the same spirit; these words apply to my little army. If a female leader commands, every normal man refuses to advance. If she leads by the "order" of requests, her entire little army advances with the precision of automata—and the force of united spirit.

On this principle I organized my little army of ten which, with its units scattered over different parts of Paris and the front, co-operated according to my wishes for united response in "united front," the latter representing an essential requisite for the success of this venture. Choosing units with extreme care, every successful military leader proceeds to infuse into the whole body the spirit of the Navy, after blending with it the Army's contribution of unwavering obedience. If masculinity, as Nature's endowment, had fallen to the writer's lot, probably she would have tried to be in the Navy, if not a member of the Law!

Precise analysis as to what caused the success of my undertaking proves an extremely difficult undertaking in itself; so far as this little venture succeeded I can only thank the little army to whom I owe success. Why each unit readily contributed his share I do not know; certainly, I am not remarkably pretty, hence power of feminine witchery found no place here! Why men helped? I do not know. Anyhow, I do say "Thank you" to each of that little band.

The day following the first night in that guard-room I felt symptoms of nervous exhaustion. With odd weakness I had fits of crying and I could hardly account for these feelings. On getting up in the

THE AUTHOR IN PRIVATE LIFE

morning I had brought to me, by a man, washing-water conveyed in collapsible pails. Before my toilet was completed, under thoroughly uncomfortable conditions, one of the officers, bearing a message, arrived at my door. He said that I must hurry up, as I was wanted.

In five minutes I was conducted downstairs to another room where, grouped around the room, sat three British Generals, one of these being Sir Charles Munro. All wore full uniform, prepared, as it seemed, to hold a private court-martial! And I represented the culprit! In the company of these Generals, several English officers, including members of the Staff, together with plainly clad khaki figures, were assembled, rather like an English jury in a London court of justice. At the small table sat a shorthand reporter. Into this great presence, including so many well-known figures, I was ushered!

Never shall I forget the ludicrous gravity on the face of one of the three Generals there; his face suggested that within my khaki-clad self abode the concentrated essence of all German spies as well as woman's natural wit. I nearly laughed. In fact I arrived on the scene wearing a broad grin. At this moment, when Allied forces were hoping that a great victory might result from the first battle of Loos, I, foolishly unimportant English girl, occupied the undivided attention of six famous Generals, together with, approximately, twenty staff officers and other officials. Though that fact suggested what was laughable, I felt, as an Englishwoman, that there seemed singular gravity in the situation; our Higher Command surely lacked imagination and proper perspective, otherwise this trivial escapade never could have assumed such proportions nor claimed this vast attention.

Long ago these officers concerned should have "summed me up"! It ought not to have taken this business to deal with one troublesome English girl. Over this matter I speak with due humility, respecting, as does every one, the wonderful bravery of our English military, while I cannot help feeling convinced that three faults reveal themselves as largely responsible for our military difficulties in the field. The mind of the soldier is ignorant of human nature, is lacking in imagination, and insufficiently intuitive or agile. It is a *set* mind.

"Don't bluff!" I felt inclined to say to this august company. "I know you are deeply worried; that I have beaten your system; that virtually *you* rest in *my* hands, not I in yours, until I choose to divulge what I decide to tell. No one possesses means to extract information from a woman. No one asks the Higher Command to 'pass under the spears' in this ludicrous case; on the other hand do not pose as conquerors over this woman who has 'caught you out' in fair game! Three forms of punishment meet this offence—only three—shooting, summons, imprisonment. None of these are available in this case. Under charge of espionage I can prove innocence; without money I should be useless if summoned; if imprisoned for the duration, I know a powerful London agency that would be effective for the instant release of this missing girl."

Before the large assembly, I knew in five minutes which one could exercise deepest initiative, if faced with an emergency, it was that red-lapelled figure, alert, smiling, human, with its legs crossed; that was Sir Charles Munro; though at the time I was unaware of his identity. As regards my own case I felt that it would have been easier first to have blocked the way I came, considering I was safely under arrest, before giving special attention to me as an individual. These hours spent by British Generals on detailed cross-examination could have been better occupied in preventing German women from following my route.

Sir Charles Munro took considerable interest, as did also one of his brother Generals, in this unique prisoner of war. But both men resolved that to show interest on this solemn occasion was beneath the laws of official discretion. Sternly implacable sat the third General; and members of the company showed various shades of interest, humour, incredulity. In the simplest manner I related the story, as I have done here, without exaggeration or attempt to deceive in any way. And here again this method puzzled my hearers in exactly the same way as bewilderment followed in the mind of that judge of German prisoners. Courtesy was shown at this cross-examination; rarely was I interrupted by questions and I simply went straight on with my story.

How long I remained in that room, as central figure of interest, it is difficult to say. I do know that no respite followed likely to relieve the irksome conditions of my captivity. On returning to the guard-room I lived as before; without a woman for any word of inquiry, without decency in sleeping accommodation! Trying to look out of the window, in hope of passing the time, I was forbidden to approach any window or look from one. Never was I allowed out of sight; and I grew to regard that guard-room as a kind of Tussaud "Chamber of Horrors." Three days and nights! Then something broke this regime. One evening I sat listlessly, as usual, watching several of the men cleaning their brass buttons; all at once the door opened, with a flourish, and there strode forward a handsome staff officer in early middle-life.

"Are you Miss Lawrence?" he inquired, smiling.

"I am," I replied.

"I am Captain X.," he said. "I have come to take you away from here."

Outside the window strolled up and down that patrol on duty night and day; and he had said, "If you try to escape you will be shot in the leg." Replying to this handsome dark officer I said :

"Oh, I *am* glad to see you!" Hearing that kind voice transformed the situation; threats only urge rebellion in certain dispositions and that threat to shoot me in the leg contrasted ill with this chivalry.

"Come along," said Captain X.

I followed, thanking the guard for the consideration shown me as I left.

Of all the strange coincidences this meeting struck me as the oddest! On leaving England I had come out, armed with *one* written introduction. That introduction happened to be to a Captain; the said Captain arranged to meet me and show me around. We failed to meet. Weeks later a Captain appeared in that guard-room. It was he! And he had overheard my name while at the officers' mess !

Very soon I had confided in this kind friend. To him I described how, following my cross-examination before the Generals, I had been sent for informally by Sir Charles Munro. "What did you do it for?" Sir Charles inquired. In conversation with Captain X. I related what reply I had given. At the outbreak of war I had volunteered twelve times for various forms of war-work; on each occasion I had been turned down, usually due to the fact that I had no money to put in canteens, neither had I experience in nursing. At the commencement of war I equipped myself as a V.A.D.; that was all. I had offered to go out where fever raged; or to anything for which I was really wanted. "We don't want anyone young"! So I was refused. Nothing came of my efforts.

At the time, war-correspondents chafed "in the leash"; they were forbidden access to the front. So I started. And I got to the front. And with two and sixpence only as my worldly wealth. I got there! There is the story. "And"—repeating what I told Sir Charles Munro—"as to the sergeant through whom I was arrested I should like to punish him if I had the strength; what he did, he achieved in so low down a manner. If he had been to a public school he would not have behaved in that way."

Sir Charles smiled. "No public schoolboy could have behaved in that manner." With those words our interview closed. But I have pleasant recollections of Sir Charles Munro; with what kindness and consideration he behaved towards me. Before I left the Third Army I asked him if I could not be kept as a despatch rider. In reply he sent a note that failed to reach its destination; just as the car drove me away I saw the orderly fluttering it in the direction of the car. But we did not stop to take that note.

Often I have wondered what it contained. Perhaps that orderly from the guard-room happened to be he who said, "No, we know you're not a spy. We are just trying to find out *what* you are!"

Captain X. showed interest in all I had to say. He happened to be acquainted with a London friend of mine; and this friend hearing I was going to France, wrote out requesting this Captain to look me up. Soon after my arrival in France, Captain X. had planned, as already explained, for us to meet; this appointment could not be kept, owing to military duties. So I had never seen this officer. On arrest, after this escapade, I refrained from asking for him. I did not wish that his name should become associated with this female desperado. On his return from leave to the Third Army Headquarters, he overheard mention of my name.

"What Miss Lawrence?" he said. "Oh, don't you know? There is a girl-prisoner here." And they told him the story.

Immediately he chivalrously claimed acquaintance with me, saying, "She must come away at once from that guardroom. Whatever she has done she is a lady. You can't treat her like that."

Protests followed from all quarters. Evidently he did not realize the full gravity of the offence, etc. etc. As reply he came without delay to the guardroom from which he took me at once. I became the Captain's prisoner of war; and I was put up in his own suite of rooms, no other being available! Strange conjunction of coincidences, indeed, that a suspected girl-spy, possessed before suspect action with personal introduction to a staff officer, meets eventually for the first time accidentally this said officer whose official work dealt almost exclusively with highest precautions against espionage! No host could have behaved with greater charm than Captain X., charged with special guard over a female prisoner of war. In conversation I learnt what the Generals, also the other officers, really thought about their prisoner.

"They simply don't know what to make of you! Such candour as yours completely disarms these men. One thinks that you are a spy; another says you must be a camp-follower; and everyone has his own views on the subject. No one guesses the truth."

"How strange! I've told the absolute truth," I said.

"Yes, that's what puzzles them. In such circumstances, it is the truth they cannot credit." He laughed. "It is your truthfulness really that causes complications."

One rather amusing complication, regarding my cross-examination, I do clearly recollect. It was generally assumed by my judges that the term "camp-follower "conveyed its own clear meaning to my mind. So, as neither prisoner nor judges discovered any hitch in the proceedings, we talked steadily at cross purposes. On my side I had not been informed what the term meant, and on their side they continued unaware that I remained ignorant! So I appeared often to be telling lies; as my judges cross-examined, with one meaning in view, and I replied, having quite another notion in my brain, we did not exactly clear up this case!

"Well, now what's to happen?" I asked.

"In the first place I've told them that I've known you for five years, and that I know your family," he explained. Splendid group of chivalrous lies; never had we met until this occasion! "Tomorrow they remove you from here."

"Where to?" I asked.

"They'll motor you to General Headquarters, St. Omer; many miles from here," he said. "In London we shall have much to talk about. But that remains in the future."

So I was to move again! Cross-examination has not yet finished. Oh, how silly it seemed to create such fuss over one adventurous girl.

Anyhow the Third Army Headquarters produced one slight change for me. I got at last into woman's clothing. Various sources managed jointly this achievement; and there came from diverse quarters a pair of corsets, furiously bunching up a figure for which they were never cut, white skirt tucked to the shape of crinoline hoops, the white cricketing cap, and Captain X.'s suspenders with his socks! Thus my little khaki outfit returned to military authorities.

One of Captain X.'s cars drove on the following morning with me to General Headquarters, St. Omer. At that time St. Omer stood many miles behind the fire zone. It was decided that I should be brought before the Provost-Marshal of the whole Army; and through him General French would pass decision as to my ultimate fate. Really I began to wonder whether, perhaps, I was the. All Highest himself—no greater attention could have been paid to the *Kaiser*! Anyhow I felt no regret; when undertaking this exploit I hoped, by its success, to make traps for German spies. In the ride to St. Omer—it occupied several hours—I furnished my guard, a courteous member of the Secret Intelligence, with whatever help I could offer as assistance in the tightening up of our system for prevention of espionage. As I said, German girls could easily follow the same route as I had come. Additional sentinels should be put on at certain spots; and also a more stringent supervision of passports be assured. I paid warm tribute to the efficiency of the French *gendarme*; through his vigilance, indeed, I had had some narrow escapes.

"Yes," said the officer. "I always feel that *gendarmes* rank amongst our best officials."

Throughout this conversation the car cut through miles of French scenery, made picturesque by rich green grass, and fringing white roads that stretched endlessly between guards of sharp-pointed poplars. As with the sudden change made in domestic life between peace days and war, so this lovely French countryside produced on its earthy surface that acute demarcation between prosperity and ruin. In Northern France, there appeared to be no medium condition between desolated country and rich fertility unspoiled as the earth gaped with shell wounds, it seemed to look upon that tranquil sky overhead with mute appeal for vengeance, and the silence of Mother Earth grew in potency by surroundings of undisturbed fertility.

During our long ride one interval occurred when, briefly asking permission, a distinguished French officer got into the front seat of the car. As to his destination I knew nothing; what attracted my attention was the manner of his departure from his troops. It seemed significant of French military tactics. This officer came up to the car, with quick and nervous tread, as though lightly picking his steps, in the manner peculiar to the French race; and his troops, falling into line, with graceful movement, yet automatic precision, stood to the salute, standing in single file one behind the other. Forty seconds completed that military send-off; in it there appeared ceremony without the delay of official function. In England there seems always so much fuss in concentrating attention exactly on conventional observances if our Generals take leave of their suite it takes far longer than forty seconds, and the departure, compared with similar occurrences in the French army, lacks graceful action and precision. This I remark only by the way.

CHAPTER 7

In a Convent

In that narrow mean street of St. Omer, town made famous by centuries of history, there drew up a car, with its incongruous modern look and its raucous hoots. And I stepped out, to blot further the landscape of wonderful buildings and summer sky, wearing that crinoline little skirt, boy's sporting hat, a staff officer's shoes, and Captain X.'s best suspenders and socks!

"You'd perhaps like to buy a few clothes here?" queried my guard; he numbered amongst the nicest of my new acquaintances.

I assented, with real pleasure. Captain X. had insisted that I should accept a temporary loan until my return across the water.

"Yes, may I?" I asked.

"Run along, then."

And I was allowed out of sight for half an hour. During that time I managed to buy shoes and stockings, though the other clothes had to do until I could get to London. As to souvenirs I kept Captain X.'s suspenders; and I have them today! As also the khaki handkerchief of a private soldier.

On arriving at headquarters my guard alighted; and after several minutes had elapsed I heard:

"No, it is all right, Miss Lawrence, you need not come in. I have arranged that for you. The Provost-Marshal will see you later."

Seeing that he had delivered his charge at headquarters, this officer, badly needed at the Third Army, prepared to take his departure. His ready courtesy won my gratitude and I offered heartfelt thanks as he left me. Coming out from headquarters, a "red tab" staff officer took his vacated place at my side. Soon I discovered that I had lost one genial companion to get this pale, cold official. His intention was to improve the shining hour by "*making hay while the sun shone*" in efforts

83

to reform this young renegade.

"I suppose you know that you are being housed at State expense?" In like manner he continued. He seemed unchivalrous in his effort to take advantage of my helpless position at the moment; fortunately, the stoppage of our car, after only a few minutes, put a stop to this staff officer's unwelcome remarks.

Looking from the car window, I saw formidable walls, resembling those of a prison, which later appeared as the exterior of Le Convent de bon Pasteur.

"You're to be placed in this convent," explained my guard.

So the end of it all meant convent life, perhaps "for the duration"! Horrors! I was to enter this place whence Sisters never left! The Convent de bon Pasteur belonged to one of the strictest Romanist orders; no nun left its precincts. "Come along!"

And I was marshalled through that great door, and shown into a small room flanked by an iron grill. This grill separated the room from all other parts of the building. Stooping down to the tiny square door, forming part of the grating, the Sister spoke; she then disappeared to inform *La Mère* of our arrival.

After some brief words between staff officer and *La Mère*, bearing on this luckless "prisoner of war," clang went the iron door, echoing its ring across stone-paved floors; I was shut off from all worldly sights and in company with this little band of holy women. With a kind smile *La Mère*, one of France's old aristocrats, led the way towards my room. I can hear in memory today that hollow sound of footfalls, clanking against stone floors! In my clean bedroom I found little distraction except in that huge Saint whoever he happened to be! He never took his eyes off me. But he was made of stone, thank goodness!

Meals came by the hand of a young novice. They were served with perfect daintiness; and I enjoyed the fresh, luscious pears, red wine, and warm milk.

Young officers called from headquarters. They spoke from behind the grating, as they handed through it for me to read *With the Allies* and another book.

Three hundred Sisters approximately, if I remember rightly, comprise the occupants of this convent. And I experienced from each woman nothing but the kindest treatment throughout the two weeks spent behind convent walls. Shyly Sisters used to seek out this young desperado of their own sex; and with the frank curiosity of children, these people asked hundreds of questions. And all about what exactly

I *had* done? Knots of black-robed figures used to gather round me on summer evenings, walking backwards along sandy walks, utterly enthralled at the adventures of a woman who had got out to the big world.

At seven o'clock one evening I sat up in bed, dressed in man's pyjamas, eating my dinner in Divisional headquarters, without one woman anywhere near; and seven o'clock on the following evening saw the same girl as centre figure of a group, where nuns crowded footpaths to hear adventurous stories in the sacred precincts of a strict Romanist order where man was anathema! Truly, life moves by quick changes, ranging with the rapidity of cinema pictures.

While at the convent I used voluntarily to attend services in the beautiful little chapel that adjoined the main building. One evening stands out in my memory. It was not associated with the services at the chapel just mentioned. It was one of those perfect evenings that seem to send a hush over all the earth, with just that tinge of foreboding sadness to remind one that autumn stands waiting with its scythe, and death awaits in readiness to gather its winter of full harvests. Such a night it was; and I remember it. Acres of fruit-garden ranged with row upon row of heavily-laden pear-trees, stretching as the background of that gaunt grey building with its rooms divided into sleeping rooms or schoolrooms—teaching at the convent school occupied the Sisters each day.

Enclosing the convent grounds a high wall, like prison walls, divided this quiet place from the noisy world outside, while, within the grounds, walking in and out between lanes of fruit trees, black and white figures cast shadows on the sun-flecked grassy slopes that led up to a huge granite crucifix. The crucifix stood fixed in the farthest corner of the convent grounds. Narrow paths interlaced in graceful curves of bright brown gravel throughout the wide grounds.

Across this scene there drifted the monotonous tone of *"Priez pour nous! Priez pour nous! Priez pour nous!"* The regular beat of these words rang on the night air, when girls, singing in the first burst of youth, chanted dolefully these three words. And with these words they kept time, as irons went up and down the linen that they were ironing. These three words alone broke the stillness until, without any previous warning, tomboyish yells from happy children, turned into the playground, drowned *"Priez pour nous!"* with cries of voices at play.

"Ah, M'delle! M'delle Anglaise!" Crowds flocked to my window, "Please, will you come out to play?"

85

"Yes! I will."

"Hooray! "they cried in real English fashion, while little human people buzzed with questions, asking whether I would say what I had done.

Then I had to display souvenirs, tell stories, explain bits of munition, and amuse! Regularly each evening I used to play in the convent yard with these little French children, and I became eventually quite a popular heroine, retiring in pomp with *"Vive l'Angleterre!"* shouted through my window by the throng of children. Dear little children! Through the bitterness of bloodshed and dirty quagmire of politics, one thing above all others I hope for England, it is that we may never fall from our pedestal established by French parents to-day in the hearts of France's little children. Times may change; and old hearts change with them. But what France thinks to-day, through the mind of her little ones, England reaps tomorrow at the hands of children grown to manhood.

"Vive l'Angleterre!" those words reverberated through the air. As the sound died, the scene reshuffled. The children went off to sleep; silently nuns took their place in the convent walks.

"Tell us what you saw at the front." And I said as much as I was permitted to say. Walking backwards along gravel walks these Sisters wandered. Such childlike eyes they possessed. They wondered at what I had to tell. Again the scene changed. Through that solemn hush with which Nature clothes the dying days of midsummer-weather, evening crept slowly with slanting shadows; at this sign the nuns gathered together in one group on the gravel paths that lay fringed with grass. They ended that day with vesper prayer. *La Mère* stepped forward from the cluster of black and white forms; slowly falling to her knees on the red gravel, the black figure, grouped about with other black figures, flung the folds of her black gown across vivid green of grass, and, with each nun, knelt with bowed head, in prayer. The blue sky faded gradually into sober grey, pushing the crucifix farther into the shadows. The sounds of Latin chants drifted across the grounds, and higher up a whir of passing friendly aeroplanes announced that Allies kept guard over prayer and children.

In school hours I felt very bored. After reading the two books I had nothing to do. So I used to visit the guinea-pigs; and I had one offered as a gift. Omer, as I called him, later returned to England, and subsequently died from spontaneous combustion! In brief, he overate himself! On two occasions English officers paid official visits. Three charming young officers, staying behind the iron bars, brought with them a paper, which I was asked to sign. I put my signature to the narrative I had given of my doings.

"I am afraid I must ask you to sign this," courteously said one officer, speaking rather apologetically.

So I signed. How quickly human animals acquire habits! As I read before signing, I found that I was caressing my short hair after the manner practised by men when they appear deep in thought! And these officers did laugh as they noticed this masculine trait! They inquired if I were comfortable in every way. And did I want anything?

"My freedom!" I said. Though within spacious grounds, I felt that these walls limited where I might walk; as with all British people, I groaned under captivity, be it ever so unfettered. On arrival my knife, too, had been taken away; that large clasp-knife! It looked so dangerous; maybe "They" feared I contemplated murder and suicide. On my exit from the convent, the knife was returned!

Time weighed heavily on my hands; occasionally I went to the nuns' room, where these ladies sat all round the room, busied with needlework for the poor. At other times I hunted for ripe pears; and they *were* juicy too! In that convent I became a sort of mascot, pampered and beloved, despite my wickedness!

In very wicked moments I used to say:

"I'll get you all out, and I'll find *husbands* for you. Here you are, stuck away here, wasting pretty faces and young lives. It is awful! And I'm stuck here just so long as any news that I may have gathered is *not* too stale for London papers; when any war news no longer is London news, I shall be released! That I quite realize. *I* see their game!" Peals of laughter: and "But we don't want husbands!" said one or two voices; other Sisters remained silent!

"After the war you will come out and stay with us, won't you?" said my hostesses.

"I will, please." And I hope to keep that promise.

Two weeks passed in the convent. Then I heard news. Lord French, or Sir John French, as he was in those days, gave orders that I should return to England.

"What shall I send you from home?" I asked the Sisters.

"Some custard powder and a big ball," came the odd reply.

I sent the powder with an English football.

Later both came back to my London address by order of the military authorities! That seemed such a pity! Why return harmless gifts, especially as the children so wanted their promised ball!

The Provost-Marshal, General Bunbury, sent for me from the convent. In a polite little note, written in his own handwriting, I heard that he, renowned General, and Provost-Marshal of the British Army, required my presence at a given hour; one of the N.C.O.'s would call for me.

Soon I confronted the sixth General I was to meet in connection with this affair. In outward manner the severity of the Provost-Marshal usually repelled, perhaps, though I felt drawn to this grave and dignified old man. With perfect courtesy this English gentleman treated me as a lady, though his seeming frigidity never unbent for one moment. In striking contrast I noticed the weather-beaten bronzed face, evidently the face of an Indian veteran, as compared with the jovial ruddy faces of the five Generals whom I had already confronted. General Bunbury said when I was to leave for England and by what route. With perfect taste he purposely revealed that he had been compelled to read the letters I had written while at the convent, yet he made the revelation without embarrassing his prisoner. He simply said:

"What made you think that you were to be kept at the convent?" referring thus to the contents of my letters!

In a few minutes my interview with the General had finished; only Islanders can appreciate what intense relief accompanies release from captivity.

I said "goodbye" to the convent. And what a splendid send-off the nuns gave on that occasion! Delightful forethought those Sisters showed. They came up with offerings of little treasures, perhaps a sacred card kept carefully for ten years, and whatever also the Sisters really valued. Omer, squeaking, packed himself into the cab, and I followed, together with the presents and an officer. One incident stands out in my mind. Nearly every soldier off duty when I left St. Omer came to give me a send-off. It was fine of them! And I did appreciate their action, though I felt the honour to be undeserved. Each soldier came to shake hands at the window of the car. So I went.

In my ear rang :

"More of us would have come, only authorities have kept rather quiet about it; not all the men know."

Anyhow I look back with gratitude to that send-off. As yet I remained "prisoner of war." Under escort I drove to Boulogne. I remained under surveillance in the shed occupied by Secret Intelligence Officers at Boulogne till time to board the boat. Unfortunately,

I looked very conspicuous with my cropped hair and "crinoline" skirt, and I could not hope to escape notice on the Channel boat. With very mixed feelings I stepped on board; one-third of my life would I have given to possess one of those "*roving* "commissions so readily afforded to accredited war-correspondents. And I did so want to do work in the war zone! Instead, here I boarded boat for home!

On the other hand, I was to go into freedom. At this juncture I wondered what "the paper," that powerful newspaper, would say on my return. Under cross-examination I had said, "Please understand that no newspaper has sent me out. I am a free lance. I only worked as unattached reporter on so-and-so paper up till the time I left for France. It is true I wanted to get news for that paper; the responsibility for this escapade rests entirely with me." Coming home without any war news, I wished that secrecy should be maintained so far as the newspaper itself was concerned; this matter looked thoroughly disreputable to anyone unacquainted with the true circumstances and with me.

People today will probably think that I must have been immoral at the front; reading this account they will say, "Pooh! of course those soldiers did not behave in that way for nothing!" They did! And I write this book as a result of British chivalry. And it was chiefly simple soldiers who showed this chivalry. From my own words I stand judged; for the sake of British and French men, whether civilian or military, I hope that I shall be believed. Upon the wide world I throw this book, confident that Truth will out; I have nothing to hide and I have told the truth.

What people think about me matters extremely little; although the chief figure in the incidents of the book I desire that in the spirit of it I may be only the background on which English soldiers, together with valued friends at home, figure as real heroes with moral combats as well as heroes when seen with guns in the field. Remember that I passed through the lines, dressed as a girl, that I lived amidst a French army, and within an English camp, that I lived two weeks under fire as a soldier, yet I return to England without any cause for regret. I echo the tribute of a Colonel, saying "*Well, I call that damn good.*" He knew the spirit of the Allied forces; and I have learnt how grandly that spirit abides.

CHAPTER 8

On Board

News of my adventure had travelled; I realized it as I got on board. And I discovered that additional interest marked this particular voyage owing to two other conspicuous figures present with me in the same boat. Mrs. Pankhurst, accompanied by another prominent suffragette, crossed over, also a Colonel, remarkable as having risen gradually from the ranks to his present position. The Colonel and I conversed at length. Also Mrs. Pankhurst came up to where I stood. She asked if I would speak at a forthcoming meeting. Later this idea was quashed by D.O.R.A.

Arriving at Folkestone I underwent cross-examination once more. Altogether it must have been ten times that I was examined. Hustle possessed Folkestone quay as the boat dropped anchor. Busy men stood behind a long bench where, parcels plumped down, every package was examined; and two women, having an equally busy time, searched female passengers, as they assembled under woodwork sheds for that formality. I was brought before a khaki officer who, typically Irish, wanted to hear full details of my escapade. This man exacted certain promises; he had some claim to respect—his youth temporarily smashed by partial paralysis all down one side, through wounds received in action. He looked what he was: an Irish hero D.S.O.; blue-eyed, humorous, brave, impulsive! Intently he listened to all I had to say. No comment openly did he make. One graceful act he offered, I thought he deliberately limped along at my side when I had to appear on the public platform; he carefully avoided that onlookers should mistake me for a captured spy.

While waiting at the quay, people showed marked kindness; canteen ladies freely "treated" me at the canteen, reserved for soldiers; one old fisherman came up and shook hands with me; people made everything as easy as possible for this short-haired "prisoner of war."

The night following my arrival in England I had to stay in Folkestone, rather I was asked if I would stay. In the typical surroundings of a fisherman's home I spent the night with Folkestone fisher-folk around; seated at the supper-table, eating my fish-supper, I heard the first English news; a Folkestone woman had cut her throat through the horror of the latest air raid! So there was no getting away from war! Residence in England only meant that people met war in one form while fighters in the firing-line met it in another form. Here, in England, people lived in perpetual peril of sudden attack by air, while soldiers in the firing-line lost any sense of wariness through their perpetual preparedness!

Before I left Folkestone one ordeal took place. In an embarrassing interview with the officer who had won the D.S.O. I promised not to divulge any information till I got permission. In making that promise I sacrificed the chance of earning by newspaper articles written on this escapade; as a girl compelled to earn her livelihood, I lost, temporarily anyhow, all material gain by that promise. One of England's heroes exacted it, and that I found worth noting. And he said:

"I ask for the sake of the country."

In the interval between my arrival at Folkestone and departure for London, telephone messages were exchanged between Scotland Yard and the young Irish officer here. The Yard was notified at what hour I was to travel; and it sent an inspector, who waited for me at the railway station. As the train steamed out from Folkestone an officer, tiptoeing on the footboard, said:

"You shall have a medal for special war service."

But it has never come! Hardly surprising! Why on earth should I have any medal for making of myself a general nuisance? To this day I feel thankful, however, that I created *useful* nuisance. Nothing noteworthy occurred till Omer and I alighted on the London platform; then there came forward immediately a tall plain-clothes detective. He took the pair of us as far as the Yard.

"You wait in the hall."

I waited, as "prisoner of war," inside Scotland Yard. He reappeared.

"All right, you need not come in." And he smiled pleasantly. "Go now, but for ten days keep us notified of your address."

No longer prisoner of war, I passed from the stone portals of Scotland Yard out to the Embankment. Just at that hour the Embankment lights dodge each other fitfully along the ever-moving waters of calm old Thames. Under my arm I held that little parcel, squeaking Omer, as practically all I had brought from France, and slowly walked along, passing begrimed tramps in wretched sleep, with heavy steps. In this big London city I do not think that anyone felt lonelier than I! Just home from the front, I had nowhere to go! No friends knew that I had come back; and my own house had been let to foreigners. So I had homelessness as immediate prospect! I had to think. Eventually I solved the problem. On some friends I would pay a call; perhaps they could put me up for the night. So I went my way—at home without a home, yet just "home" from the front.

Written in April 1918.

LEONAUR

ALSO FROM LEONAUR

AVAILABLE IN SOFTCOVER OR HARDCOVER WITH DUST JACKET

THE FALL OF THE MOGHUL EMPIRE OF HINDUSTAN *by H. G. Keene*—By the beginning of the nineteenth century, as British and Indian armies under Lake and Wellesley dominated the scene, a little over half a century of conflict brought the Moghul Empire to its knees.

LADY SALE'S AFGHANISTAN *by Florentia Sale*—An Indomitable Victorian Lady's Account of the Retreat from Kabul During the First Afghan War.

THE CAMPAIGN OF MAGENTA AND SOLFERINO 1859 *by Harold Carmichael Wylly*—The Decisive Conflict for the Unification of Italy.

FRENCH'S CAVALRY CAMPAIGN *by J. G. Maydon*—A Special Correspondent's View of British Army Mounted Troops During the Boer War.

CAVALRY AT WATERLOO *by Sir Evelyn Wood*—British Mounted Troops During the Campaign of 1815.

THE SUBALTERN *by George Robert Gleig*—The Experiences of an Officer of the 85th Light Infantry During the Peninsular War.

NAPOLEON AT BAY, 1814 *by F. Loraine Petre*—The Campaigns to the Fall of the First Empire.

NAPOLEON AND THE CAMPAIGN OF 1806 *by Colonel Vachée*—The Napoleonic Method of Organisation and Command to the Battles of Jena & Auerstädt.

THE COMPLETE ADVENTURES IN THE CONNAUGHT RANGERS *by William Grattan*—The 88th Regiment during the Napoleonic Wars by a Serving Officer.

BUGLER AND OFFICER OF THE RIFLES *by William Green & Harry Smith*—With the 95th (Rifles) during the Peninsular & Waterloo Campaigns of the Napoleonic Wars.

NAPOLEONIC WAR STORIES *by Sir Arthur Quiller-Couch*—Tales of soldiers, spies, battles & sieges from the Peninsular & Waterloo campaigns.

CAPTAIN OF THE 95TH (RIFLES) *by Jonathan Leach*—An officer of Wellington's sharpshooters during the Peninsular, South of France and Waterloo campaigns of the Napoleonic wars.

RIFLEMAN COSTELLO *by Edward Costello*—The adventures of a soldier of the 95th (Rifles) in the Peninsular & Waterloo Campaigns of the Napoleonic wars.

LEONAUR

ALSO FROM LEONAUR
AVAILABLE IN SOFTCOVER OR HARDCOVER WITH DUST JACKET

AT THEM WITH THE BAYONET *by Donald F. Featherstone*—The first Anglo-Sikh War 1845-1846.

STEPHEN CRANE'S BATTLES *by Stephen Crane*—Nine Decisive Battles Recounted by the Author of 'The Red Badge of Courage'.

THE GURKHA WAR *by H. T. Prinsep*—The Anglo-Nepalese Conflict in North East India 1814-1816.

FIRE & BLOOD *by G. R. Gleig*—The burning of Washington & the battle of New Orleans, 1814, through the eyes of a young British soldier.

SOUND ADVANCE! *by Joseph Anderson*—Experiences of an officer of HM 50th regiment in Australia, Burma & the Gwalior war.

THE CAMPAIGN OF THE INDUS *by Thomas Holdsworth*—Experiences of a British Officer of the 2nd (Queen's Royal) Regiment in the Campaign to Place Shah Shuja on the Throne of Afghanistan 1838 - 1840.

WITH THE MADRAS EUROPEAN REGIMENT IN BURMA *by John Butler*—The Experiences of an Officer of the Honourable East India Company's Army During the First Anglo-Burmese War 1824 - 1826.

IN ZULULAND WITH THE BRITISH ARMY *by Charles L. Norris-Newman*—The Anglo-Zulu war of 1879 through the first-hand experiences of a special correspondent.

BESIEGED IN LUCKNOW *by Martin Richard Gubbins*—The first Anglo-Sikh War 1845-1846.

A TIGER ON HORSEBACK *by L. March Phillips*—The Experiences of a Trooper & Officer of Rimington's Guides - The Tigers - during the Anglo-Boer war 1899 - 1902.

SEPOYS, SIEGE & STORM *by Charles John Griffiths*—The Experiences of a young officer of H.M.'s 61st Regiment at Ferozepore, Delhi ridge and at the fall of Delhi during the Indian mutiny 1857.

CAMPAIGNING IN ZULULAND *by W. E. Montague*—Experiences on campaign during the Zulu war of 1879 with the 94th Regiment.

THE STORY OF THE GUIDES *by G.J. Younghusband*—The Exploits of the Soldiers of the famous Indian Army Regiment from the northwest frontier 1847 - 1900.

ALSO FROM LEONAUR

AVAILABLE IN SOFTCOVER OR HARDCOVER WITH DUST JACKET

ZULU:1879 *by D.C.F. Moodie & the Leonaur Editors*—The Anglo-Zulu War of 1879 from contemporary sources: First Hand Accounts, Interviews, Dispatches, Official Documents & Newspaper Reports.

THE RED DRAGOON *by W.J. Adams*—With the 7th Dragoon Guards in the Cape of Good Hope against the Boers & the Kaffir tribes during the 'war of the axe' 1843-48'.

THE RECOLLECTIONS OF SKINNER OF SKINNER'S HORSE *by James Skinner*—James Skinner and his 'Yellow Boys' Irregular cavalry in the wars of India between the British, Mahratta, Rajput, Mogul, Sikh & Pindarree Forces.

A CAVALRY OFFICER DURING THE SEPOY REVOLT *by A. R. D. Mackenzie*—Experiences with the 3rd Bengal Light Cavalry, the Guides and Sikh Irregular Cavalry from the outbreak to Delhi and Lucknow.

A NORFOLK SOLDIER IN THE FIRST SIKH WAR *by J W Baldwin*—Experiences of a private of H.M. 9th Regiment of Foot in the battles for the Punjab, India 1845-6.

TOMMY ATKINS' WAR STORIES: 14 FIRST HAND ACCOUNTS—Fourteen first hand accounts from the ranks of the British Army during Queen Victoria's Empire.

THE WATERLOO LETTERS *by H. T. Siborne*—Accounts of the Battle by British Officers for its Foremost Historian.

NEY: GENERAL OF CAVALRY VOLUME 1—1769-1799 *by Antoine Bulos*—The Early Career of a Marshal of the First Empire.

NEY: MARSHAL OF FRANCE VOLUME 2—1799-1805 *by Antoine Bulos*—The Early Career of a Marshal of the First Empire.

AIDE-DE-CAMP TO NAPOLEON *by Philippe-Paul de Ségur*—For anyone interested in the Napoleonic Wars this book, written by one who was intimate with the strategies and machinations of the Emperor, will be essential reading.

TWILIGHT OF EMPIRE *by Sir Thomas Ussher & Sir George Cockburn*—Two accounts of Napoleon's Journeys in Exile to Elba and St. Helena: Narrative of Events by Sir Thomas Ussher & Napoleon's Last Voyage: Extract of a diary by Sir George Cockburn.

PRIVATE WHEELER *by William Wheeler*—The letters of a soldier of the 51st Light Infantry during the Peninsular War & at Waterloo.

AVAILABLE ONLINE AT www.leonaur.com
AND FROM ALL GOOD BOOK STORES   07/09

LEONAUR

ALSO FROM LEONAUR
AVAILABLE IN SOFTCOVER OR HARDCOVER WITH DUST JACKET

OFFICERS & GENTLEMEN *by Peter Hawker & William Graham*—Two Accounts of British Officers During the Peninsula War: Officer of Light Dragoons by Peter Hawker & Campaign in Portugal and Spain by William Graham .

THE WALCHEREN EXPEDITION *by Anonymous*—The Experiences of a British Officer of the 81st Regt. During the Campaign in the Low Countries of 1809.

LADIES OF WATERLOO *by Charlotte A. Eaton, Magdalene de Lancey & Juana Smith*—The Experiences of Three Women During the Campaign of 1815: Waterloo Days by Charlotte A. Eaton, A Week at Waterloo by Magdalene de Lancey & Juana's Story by Juana Smith.

JOURNAL OF AN OFFICER IN THE KING'S GERMAN LEGION *by John Frederick Hering*—Recollections of Campaigning During the Napoleonic Wars.

JOURNAL OF AN ARMY SURGEON IN THE PENINSULAR WAR *by Charles Boutflower*—The Recollections of a British Army Medical Man on Campaign During the Napoleonic Wars.

ON CAMPAIGN WITH MOORE AND WELLINGTON *by Anthony Hamilton*—The Experiences of a Soldier of the 43rd Regiment During the Peninsular War.

THE ROAD TO AUSTERLITZ *by R. G. Burton*—Napoleon's Campaign of 1805.

SOLDIERS OF NAPOLEON *by A. J. Doisy De Villargennes & Arthur Chuquet*—The Experiences of the Men of the French First Empire: Under the Eagles by A. J. Doisy De Villargennes & Voices of 1812 by Arthur Chuquet .

INVASION OF FRANCE, 1814 *by F. W. O. Maycock*—The Final Battles of the Napoleonic First Empire.

LEIPZIG—A CONFLICT OF TITANS *by Frederic Shoberl*—A Personal Experience of the 'Battle of the Nations' During the Napoleonic Wars, October 14th-19th, 1813.

SLASHERS *by Charles Cadell*—The Campaigns of the 28th Regiment of Foot During the Napoleonic Wars by a Serving Officer.

BATTLE IMPERIAL *by Charles William Vane*—The Campaigns in Germany & France for the Defeat of Napoleon 1813-1814.

SWIFT & BOLD *by Gibbes Rigaud*—The 60th Rifles During the Peninsula War.

ALSO FROM LEONAUR
AVAILABLE IN SOFTCOVER OR HARDCOVER WITH DUST JACKET

ADVENTURES OF A YOUNG RIFLEMAN *by Johann Christian Maempel*—The Experiences of a Saxon in the French & British Armies During the Napoleonic Wars.

THE HUSSAR *by Norbert Landsheit & G. R. Gleig*—A German Cavalryman in British Service Throughout the Napoleonic Wars.

RECOLLECTIONS OF THE PENINSULA *by Moyle Sherer*—An Officer of the 34th Regiment of Foot—'The Cumberland Gentlemen'—on Campaign Against Napoleon's French Army in Spain.

MARINE OF REVOLUTION & CONSULATE *by Moreau de Jonnès*—The Recollections of a French Soldier of the Revolutionary Wars 1791-1804.

GENTLEMEN IN RED *by John Dobbs & Robert Knowles*—Two Accounts of British Infantry Officers During the Peninsular War Recollections of an Old 52nd Man by John Dobbs An Officer of Fusiliers by Robert Knowles.

CORPORAL BROWN'S CAMPAIGNS IN THE LOW COUNTRIES *by Robert Brown*—Recollections of a Coldstream Guard in the Early Campaigns Against Revolutionary France 1793-1795.

THE 7TH (QUEENS OWN) HUSSARS: Volume 2—1793-1815 *by C. R. B. Barrett*—During the Campaigns in the Low Countries & the Peninsula and Waterloo Campaigns of the Napoleonic Wars.Volume 2: 1793-1815.

THE MARENGO CAMPAIGN 1800 *by Herbert H. Sargent*—The Victory that Completed the Austrian Defeat in Italy.

DONALDSON OF THE 94TH—SCOTS BRIGADE *by Joseph Donaldson*—The Recollections of a Soldier During the Peninsula & South of France Campaigns of the Napoleonic Wars.

A CONSCRIPT FOR EMPIRE *by Philippe as told to Johann Christian Maempel*—The Experiences of a Young German Conscript During the Napoleonic Wars.

JOURNAL OF THE CAMPAIGN OF 1815 *by Alexander Cavalié Mercer*—The Experiences of an Officer of the Royal Horse Artillery During the Waterloo Campaign.

NAPOLEON'S CAMPAIGNS IN POLAND 1806-7 *by Robert Wilson*—The campaign in Poland from the Russian side of the conflict.

AVAILABLE ONLINE AT www.leonaur.com
AND FROM ALL GOOD BOOK STORES   07/09

LEONAUR

ALSO FROM LEONAUR
AVAILABLE IN SOFTCOVER OR HARDCOVER WITH DUST JACKET

BUGEAUD: A PACK WITH A BATON *by Thomas Robert Bugeaud*—The Early Campaigns of a Soldier of Napoleon's Army Who Would Become a Marshal of France.

WATERLOO RECOLLECTIONS *by Frederick Llewellyn*—Rare First Hand Accounts, Letters, Reports and Retellings from the Campaign of 1815.

SERGEANT NICOL *by Daniel Nicol*—The Experiences of a Gordon Highlander During the Napoleonic Wars in Egypt, the Peninsula and France.

THE JENA CAMPAIGN: 1806 *by F. N. Maude*—The Twin Battles of Jena & Auerstadt Between Napoleon's French and the Prussian Army.

PRIVATE O'NEIL *by Charles O'Neil*—The recollections of an Irish Rogue of H. M. 28th Regt.—The Slashers—during the Peninsula & Waterloo campaigns of the Napoleonic war.

ROYAL HIGHLANDER *by James Anton*—A soldier of H.M 42nd (Royal) Highlanders during the Peninsular, South of France & Waterloo Campaigns of the Napoleonic Wars.

CAPTAIN BLAZE *by Elzéar Blaze*—Life in Napoleons Army.

LEJEUNE VOLUME 1 *by Louis-François Lejeune*—The Napoleonic Wars through the Experiences of an Officer on Berthier's Staff.

LEJEUNE VOLUME 2 *by Louis-François Lejeune*—The Napoleonic Wars through the Experiences of an Officer on Berthier's Staff.

CAPTAIN COIGNET *by Jean-Roch Coignet*—A Soldier of Napoleon's Imperial Guard from the Italian Campaign to Russia and Waterloo.

FUSILIER COOPER *by John S. Cooper*—Experiences in the 7th (Royal) Fusiliers During the Peninsular Campaign of the Napoleonic Wars and the American Campaign to New Orleans.

FIGHTING NAPOLEON'S EMPIRE *by Joseph Anderson*—The Campaigns of a British Infantryman in Italy, Egypt, the Peninsular & the West Indies During the Napoleonic Wars.

CHASSEUR BARRES *by Jean-Baptiste Barres*—The experiences of a French Infantryman of the Imperial Guard at Austerlitz, Jena, Eylau, Friedland, in the Peninsular, Lutzen, Bautzen, Zinnwald and Hanau during the Napoleonic Wars.

LEONAUR

ALSO FROM LEONAUR
AVAILABLE IN SOFTCOVER OR HARDCOVER WITH DUST JACKET

CAPTAIN COIGNET *by Jean-Roch Coignet*—A Soldier of Napoleon's Imperial Guard from the Italian Campaign to Russia and Waterloo.

HUSSAR ROCCA *by Albert Jean Michel de Rocca*—A French cavalry officer's experiences of the Napoleonic Wars and his views on the Peninsular Campaigns against the Spanish, British And Guerilla Armies.

MARINES TO 95TH (RIFLES) *by Thomas Fernyhough*—The military experiences of Robert Fernyhough during the Napoleonic Wars.

LIGHT BOB *by Robert Blakeney*—The experiences of a young officer in H.M 28th & 36th regiments of the British Infantry during the Peninsular Campaign of the Napoleonic Wars 1804 - 1814.

WITH WELLINGTON'S LIGHT CAVALRY *by William Tomkinson*—The Experiences of an officer of the 16th Light Dragoons in the Peninsular and Waterloo campaigns of the Napoleonic Wars.

SERGEANT BOURGOGNE *by Adrien Bourgogne*—With Napoleon's Imperial Guard in the Russian Campaign and on the Retreat from Moscow 1812 - 13.

SURTEES OF THE 95TH (RIFLES) *by William Surtees*—A Soldier of the 95th (Rifles) in the Peninsular campaign of the Napoleonic Wars.

SWORDS OF HONOUR *by Henry Newbolt & Stanley L. Wood*—The Careers of Six Outstanding Officers from the Napoleonic Wars, the Wars for India and the American Civil War.

ENSIGN BELL IN THE PENINSULAR WAR *by George Bell*—The Experiences of a young British Soldier of the 34th Regiment 'The Cumberland Gentlemen' in the Napoleonic wars.

HUSSAR IN WINTER *by Alexander Gordon*—A British Cavalry Officer during the retreat to Corunna in the Peninsular campaign of the Napoleonic Wars.

THE COMPLEAT RIFLEMAN HARRIS *by Benjamin Harris as told to and transcribed by Captain Henry Curling, 52nd Regt. of Foot*—The adventures of a soldier of the 95th (Rifles) during the Peninsular Campaign of the Napoleonic Wars.

THE ADVENTURES OF A LIGHT DRAGOON *by George Farmer & G.R. Gleig*—A cavalryman during the Peninsular & Waterloo Campaigns, in captivity & at the siege of Bhurtpore, India.

LEONAUR

ALSO FROM LEONAUR
AVAILABLE IN SOFTCOVER OR HARDCOVER WITH DUST JACKET

THE LIFE OF THE REAL BRIGADIER GERARD VOLUME 1—THE YOUNG HUSSAR 1782-1807 *by Jean-Baptiste De Marbot*—A French Cavalryman Of the Napoleonic Wars at Marengo, Austerlitz, Jena, Eylau & Friedland.

THE LIFE OF THE REAL BRIGADIER GERARD VOLUME 2—IMPERIAL AIDE-DE-CAMP 1807-1811 *by Jean-Baptiste De Marbot*—A French Cavalryman of the Napoleonic Wars at Saragossa, Landshut, Eckmuhl, Ratisbon, Aspern-Essling, Wagram, Busaco & Torres Vedras.

THE LIFE OF THE REAL BRIGADIER GERARD VOLUME 3—COLONEL OF CHASSEURS 1811-1815 *by Jean-Baptiste De Marbot*—A French Cavalryman in the retreat from Moscow, Lutzen, Bautzen, Katzbach, Leipzig, Hanau & Waterloo.

THE INDIAN WAR OF 1864 *by Eugene Ware*—The Experiences of a Young Officer of the 7th Iowa Cavalry on the Western Frontier During the Civil War.

THE MARCH OF DESTINY *by Charles E. Young & V. Devinny*—Dangers of the Trail in 1865 by Charles E. Young & The Story of a Pioneer by V. Devinny, two Accounts of Early Emigrants to Colorado.

CROSSING THE PLAINS *by William Audley Maxwell*—A First Hand Narrative of the Early Pioneer Trail to California in 1857.

CHIEF OF SCOUTS *by William F. Drannan*—A Pilot to Emigrant and Government Trains, Across the Plains of the Western Frontier.

THIRTY-ONE YEARS ON THE PLAINS AND IN THE MOUNTAINS *by William F. Drannan*—William Drannan was born to be a pioneer, hunter, trapper and wagon train guide during the momentous days of the Great American West.

THE INDIAN WARS VOLUNTEER *by William Thompson*—Recollections of the Conflict Against the Snakes, Shoshone, Bannocks, Modocs and Other Native Tribes of the American North West.

THE 4TH TENNESSEE CAVALRY *by George B. Guild*—The Services of Smith's Regiment of Confederate Cavalry by One of its Officers.

COLONEL WORTHINGTON'S SHILOH *by T. Worthington*—The Tennessee Campaign, 1862, by an Officer of the Ohio Volunteers.

FOUR YEARS IN THE SADDLE *by W. L. Curry*—The History of the First Regiment Ohio Volunteer Cavalry in the American Civil War.

LEONAUR

ALSO FROM LEONAUR
AVAILABLE IN SOFTCOVER OR HARDCOVER WITH DUST JACKET

LEONAUR

ALSO FROM LEONAUR
AVAILABLE IN SOFTCOVER OR HARDCOVER WITH DUST JACKET

IRON TIMES WITH THE GUARDS *by An O. E. (G. P. A. Fildes)*—The Experiences of an Officer of the Coldstream Guards on the Western Front During the First World War.

THE GREAT WAR IN THE MIDDLE EAST: 1 *by W. T. Massey*—The Desert Campaigns & How Jerusalem Was Won---two classic accounts in one volume.

THE GREAT WAR IN THE MIDDLE EAST: 2 *by W. T. Massey*—Allenby's Final Triumph.

SMITH-DORRIEN *by Horace Smith-Dorrien*—Isandlwhana to the Great War.

1914 *by Sir John French*—The Early Campaigns of the Great War by the British Commander.

GRENADIER *by E. R. M. Fryer*—The Recollections of an Officer of the Grenadier Guards throughout the Great War on the Western Front.

BATTLE, CAPTURE & ESCAPE *by George Pearson*—The Experiences of a Canadian Light Infantryman During the Great War.

DIGGERS AT WAR *by R. Hugh Knyvett & G. P. Cuttriss*—"Over There" With the Australians by R. Hugh Knyvett and Over the Top With the Third Australian Division by G. P. Cuttriss. Accounts of Australians During the Great War in the Middle East, at Gallipoli and on the Western Front.

HEAVY FIGHTING BEFORE US *by George Brenton Laurie*—The Letters of an Officer of the Royal Irish Rifles on the Western Front During the Great War.

THE CAMELIERS *by Oliver Hogue*—A Classic Account of the Australians of the Imperial Camel Corps During the First World War in the Middle East.

RED DUST *by Donald Black*—A Classic Account of Australian Light Horsemen in Palestine During the First World War.

THE LEAN, BROWN MEN *by Angus Buchanan*—Experiences in East Africa During the Great War with the 25th Royal Fusiliers—the Legion of Frontiersmen.

THE NIGERIAN REGIMENT IN EAST AFRICA *by W. D. Downes*—On Campaign During the Great War 1916-1918.

THE 'DIE-HARDS' IN SIBERIA *by John Ward*—With the Middlesex Regiment Against the Bolsheviks 1918-19.

LEONAUR

ALSO FROM LEONAUR
AVAILABLE IN SOFTCOVER OR HARDCOVER WITH DUST JACKET

FARAWAY CAMPAIGN *by F. James*—Experiences of an Indian Army Cavalry Officer in Persia & Russia During the Great War.

REVOLT IN THE DESERT *by T. E. Lawrence*—An account of the experiences of one remarkable British officer's war from his own perspective.

MACHINE-GUN SQUADRON *by A. M. G.*—The 20th Machine Gunners from British Yeomanry Regiments in the Middle East Campaign of the First World War.

A GUNNER'S CRUSADE *by Antony Bluett*—The Campaign in the Desert, Palestine & Syria as Experienced by the Honourable Artillery Company During the Great War .

DESPATCH RIDER *by W. H. L. Watson*—The Experiences of a British Army Motorcycle Despatch Rider During the Opening Battles of the Great War in Europe.

TIGERS ALONG THE TIGRIS *by E. J. Thompson*—The Leicestershire Regiment in Mesopotamia During the First World War.

HEARTS & DRAGONS *by Charles R. M. F. Crutwell*—The 4th Royal Berkshire Regiment in France and Italy During the Great War, 1914-1918.

INFANTRY BRIGADE: 1914 *by John Ward*—The Diary of a Commander of the 15th Infantry Brigade, 5th Division, British Army, During the Retreat from Mons.

DOING OUR 'BIT' *by Ian Hay*—Two Classic Accounts of the Men of Kitchener's 'New Army' During the Great War including *The First 100,000* & *All In It*.

AN EYE IN THE STORM *by Arthur Ruhl*—An American War Correspondent's Experiences of the First World War from the Western Front to Gallipoli-and Beyond.

STAND & FALL *by Joe Cassells*—With the Middlesex Regiment Against the Bolsheviks 1918-19.

RIFLEMAN MACGILL'S WAR *by Patrick MacGill*—A Soldier of the London Irish During the Great War in Europe including *The Amateur Army*, *The Red Horizon* & *The Great Push*.

WITH THE GUNS *by C. A. Rose & Hugh Dalton*—Two First Hand Accounts of British Gunners at War in Europe During World War 1- Three Years in France with the Guns and With the British Guns in Italy.

THE BUSH WAR DOCTOR *by Robert V. Dolbey*—The Experiences of a British Army Doctor During the East African Campaign of the First World War.

CPSIA information can be obtained
at www.ICGtesting.com
Printed in the USA
BVHW07s2054120918
527339BV00002B/48/P

9 780857 061355